Write
Away

A handbook for
YOUNG WRITERS and LEARNERS

Teacher's Guide
to the handbook

. . . a teacher's guide to accompany

Write
Away

WRITE SOURCE

GREAT SOURCE EDUCATION GROUP

a Houghton Mifflin Company
Wilmington, Massachusetts

Write Away
About the Teacher's Guide

It's important for you to know a few things about your *Write Away Teacher's Guide* before you begin to use it.

Previewing ● The opening section provides a quick tour of the handbook to help you become familiar with its basic features. The next section—"Getting Started Activities"—contains guidelines and reproducible activity sheets that you can use to introduce the handbook to your students.

Planning ● "Using *Write Away* in the Classroom" provides a variety of ideas for planning instruction. The next three sections contain summaries for all of the handbook chapters related to writing and learning skills. The "Handbook Minilessons" section contains a variety of activities to use along with the handbook. (At least one minilesson is provided for each handbook chapter.)

Managing ● "Evaluating/Assessing/Monitoring" offers suggestions for evaluating writing, basic-skills instruction, and extended units. Also included in this section is valuable information related to peer conferencing and portfolio assessment.

Supplementing ● The final sections in the *Teacher's Guide* serve as a resource for improving instruction with the handbook. "Reading-Writing Connection" lists high-interest trade books related to major chapters in the handbook. These lists can help when planning extended units. The "Bibliography" section lists additional resources for each chapter, which may also help during planning. Finally, "Program Overview" highlights the coordinating program for grade 2.

Authors: Dave Kemper, Ruth Nathan, and Carol Elsholz

Printed in the United States of America

International Standard Book Number: 0-669-44045-0

1 2 3 4 5 6 7 8 9 10 -POO- 02 01 00 99 98 97 96

What You'll Find Inside

A QUICK Tour

Write Away Student Handbook

Write Away serves as the perfect language handbook for grade 2, one that will help your students improve their ability **to write** (prewriting through proofreading), and **to learn** (in the classroom, in small groups, independently). This quick tour will highlight the handbook's major points of interest.

1 The Process of Writing

Students will use this section of the handbook to answer their questions about writing, from selecting a subject to proofreading a final draft.

36

Revising **TIPS**

Follow these tips when you revise:

READ your first draft.

LOOK for parts that could be better.

HAVE your teacher or another person read your first draft, too.

FIND OUT what your reader likes. Find out what questions he or she has.

20

Using the Writing Process

There are five steps in the writing process. Follow these steps when you write.

2 WRITE
Write about your subject.
Don't worry

21

3 REVISE
Read over your writing.
Change parts to make it better.

4 CHECK
Check for . . .
* Spelling
* Capital Letters
* Punctuation

5 PUBLISH
Write a neat copy to share. (See pages 42-47 for more ideas.)

13

Starting to Write

Why are these kids smiling? They know all about writing. And guess what? They want to share some of their ideas. Let's see what they have to say.

Colorful illustrations and a personal tone are used throughout *Write Away*. Step-by-step instructions, helpful guidelines, and checklists make information easy to find and use.

2 The Forms of Writing

When students are ready to start a personal journal, write a poem, or create a fable, this is the section to turn to.

118

Writing Reports

John Walker learned three things about his favorite dinosaur: *how big it was, what it ate,* and *where it lived.* Then he wrote a report about this information. You can read his report on page 123.

Finding and Sharing

Do you know how to find information about a subject? We will show you how in this chapter. We will also show you ways to report on what you find out.

134

Writing Add-On Stories

Stories like "The Very Enormous Turnip" and "Stone Soup" are called add-on stories. Add-on stories are fun to read and fun to write.

The Working Parts

In an **add-on story**, the main character has a problem. One by one, different characters are added to the story. A ...ppens in the end, and the ...solved.

153

Making Friends with Small Poems

Follow these tips when you read small poems.

READ the poem two or three times.

READ it aloud and listen to the sounds.

SHARE the poem with a partner.

COPY the poem into your notebook.

> **Which words help you see pictures?**
> **Which words tell feelings?**

Write Away **addresses many forms of writing, from directions to mysteries.**

3 The Tools of Learning

If your students' study, reading, or test-taking skills could use a little pumping up, have them turn to "The Tools of Learning."

180

Reading to Understand

Funny stories make you laugh. Special poems make you feel good. And interesting fact books make you a little smarter!

Planning to Learn

This chapter will help you read fact books. Each page lists a new plan that will help you read, learn, and remember.

243

Test-Taking TIPS

WRITE your name on your paper.

FOLLOW along as your teacher goes over the directions.

ASK questions if you do not understand something.

ANSWER the questions you know.

SKIP over the ones you're not sure of.

Then **GO BACK** to the unanswered questions.

> Check to make sure you answered all the questions.

228

Giving Oral Reports

Do you have a collection? Do you know how to make something? Have you just read about an interesting subject?

Telling and Showing

You can share your special information in an oral report. An **oral report** is part telling and part showing. You tell important facts about your subject. And you show pictures or examples to go with the facts.

Write Away **contains lots of easy-to-use ideas for making all aspects of language and learning active, enjoyable, and meaningful.**

Whenever students have a question about punctuation, spelling, or capitalization, they can turn to the yellow pages for help.

247

Using Punctuation

A "walk" signal tells us to go. A "don't walk" signal tells us to stop. These signals are very important.

Stopping and Going

Punctuation marks are signals we use in writing. For example, we use a period to signal a stop at the end of a sentence. You can learn about using punctuation in this chapter.

268

Using the Right Word

Some words sound alike, but they have different spellings. They also have different meanings. These words are called **homophones**.

ant	An ant crawled onto my finger.
aunt	My aunt likes to tell jokes.
ate	Liz ate lunch with me.
eight	I have eight crayons.

276

Understanding Our Language

All of the words we use fit into eight groups. These groups are called the **parts of speech**.

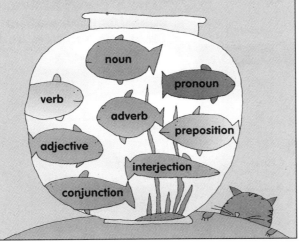

noun
pronoun
verb
adverb
preposition
adjective
interjection
conjunction

This guide to spelling, usage, punctuation, and capitalization answers your students' proofreading questions.

5 The Student Almanac

Full-color maps, a historical time line, the metric system—*Write Away* is truly an all-school handbook!

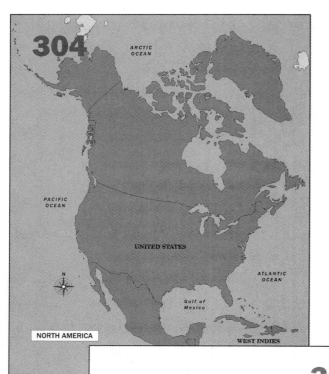

304 NORTH AMERICA

ARCTIC OCEAN

PACIFIC OCEAN

UNITED STATES

ATLANTIC OCEAN

Gulf of Mexico

WEST INDIES

308

Working with Math

You use math a lot. You add and subtract numbers, you count money, and you tell time. You also measure things, and so on.

From Adding to Telling Time

This chapter will help you become "math smart." The first part shows you how to solve word problems. The second part gives helpful math tables and charts.

"The Student Almanac" contains information useful for math, science, and social studies classes.

323

U.S. History

1607
English settle Jamestown, Virginia.

1620
Pilgrims settle Plymouth Colony.

1621
Squanto helps Pilgrims plant corn.
The first Thanksgiving is celebrated.

| 1600 | 1620 | 1640 | 1660 | 1680 |

1647
The first U.S. public schools are set up.

1622
January 1 is accepted as the beginning of the year.

1690
The first U.S. paper money is used.

Discoveries and Daily Life

Getting Started ACTIVITIES

Write Away was developed by experienced teachers and writers for students in second grade and beyond. More than anything else, we wanted to put together a handbook that students would find very helpful and very enjoyable to use. Over the past several years, teachers have told us what they like best about our other handbooks, and what they do when the book is first put into the hands of their students.

Learning About the Handbook

Many of their suggestions, plus some of our own, are contained in this section of your *Teacher's Guide*. Of special interest to you will be the suggested sequences of activities (page 11) for introducing the handbook to your students and the reproducible activity sheets on pages 12-19.

About the **Write Away** Handbook

Write Away serves as the perfect resource for students in grade 2, helping them develop their writing and learning skills. Here are four important ways that the handbook can be used:

1. Core Program Resource

Students use the handbook to help them complete the activities in the *Write Away Language Series* program. (The handbook and coordinating program can serve as the foundation for an exciting research-based language arts curriculum.)

2. Writing Guide

Students can also use the handbook to help them carry out their writing assignments in all areas of instruction, including reading/literature, social studies, science, and so on.

3. All-School Handbook

Whether students are reading in a content area, building vocabulary skills, studying maps, working in groups, or taking tests, they will find help in the *Write Away* handbook. It can assist them in all areas of the curriculum.

4. Study Helper

When students are writing or studying at home, *Write Away* will help them complete their work. Young learners (and their parents) will especially appreciate all of the handy word lists, guidelines, and models in the handbook.

Start-Up Ideas

*Use the ideas listed on the next two pages to help your students learn about and use **Write Away**.*

Scavenger Hunts

Create scavenger hunts asking students to find facts or ideas listed in the handbook. Scavenger hunts can be implemented individually in daily language practice activities or in extended activities, in which you provide students with a series of questions to answer. (See the reproducible scavenger hunts on pages 16-18 in this section.)

Example Scavenger Hunts:

* **Turn to page 42. On this page, who wrote a story of his life?**

* **Turn to the table of contents. Which page would you turn to in order to find out about journal writing?**

Reproducible Activities

Implement some of the reproducible activity sheets provided for you in this section.

One Point of Interest

Give your students the following assignment: Find one page, chart, illustration, or model that you really like or think is very important. (Students should be prepared to share their discoveries with a small group of classmates or with the entire class.)

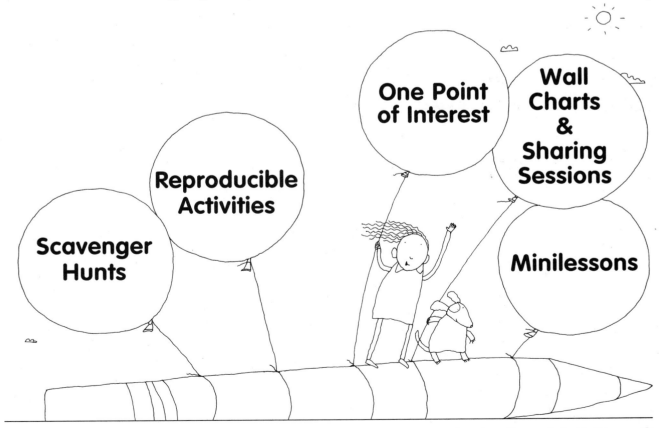

Wall Charts

Have small groups of students make wall charts based on helpful lists or guidelines contained in *Write Away*. (The "Revising Tips" on page 36 is an example.) Display the finished products in the classroom as well as in other rooms in the school.

Sharing Sessions

At different times, have students share the positive experiences they have using the handbook. For example, they might tell how the spelling lists starting on page 260 helped them, or how they discovered on page 43 that they could publish their writing by putting on a puppet show.

Minilessons

Conduct minilessons on a regular basis to give your students practice using *Write Away*. We think of minilessons as activities that can be completed in 10-15 minutes.

It's fun to write. . . . . **Starting to Write**

OPEN your handbook to page 13. The kids are smiling about writing. **TELL** what you like about writing. Or **WRITE** a few sentences telling what you like about writing.

A Cluster of Ideas . . . . **The Writing Process**

READ about clusters on page 22 of your handbook. Now try to use a cluster to plan your own writing. First **CHOOSE** a subject you would like to write about. Then fill in details around it.

Your First Week with
Write Away

Day 1

Hand out copies of *Write Away*. Invite your students to browse through their books. Ask them to share pages or pictures they especially like. Then read and discuss the poem "Books to Grow In" on page 8 in the handbook. Have students color and decorate the blackline master "Write Away for You" (page 12 in this section) after your discussion.

Day 2

Introduce students to the five main parts in *Write Away*. To begin this discussion, read page 3 in the handbook. Use the blackline master "Up, Up, and Away!" (page 13) during the discussion or as a follow-up activity.

Day 3

Discuss the table of contents with your students. Then hand out the blackline master "Getting to Know your Handbook" (page 14). This will give the children practice using the table of contents.

Day 4

Explore "Starting to Write" (pages 13-19 in *Write Away*) with your students. Read each page together. Then ask for your students' comments and reactions. Assign the blackline master "Good Ideas About Writing" (page 15) as an independent or small-group activity.

Day 5

Conduct scavenger hunts. Distribute one (or more) of the scavenger hunts (pages 16-18) for students to complete. These activities help students get to know different parts of the handbook. (The *Special Challenge* at the end of each scavenger hunt introduces students to the handbook index.)

Note: Continue reading, sharing, and learning about different parts of the handbook from week to week throughout the school year.

Write Away for You

DIRECTIONS: Read this poem from your handbook. Then have fun coloring and decorating this page.

BOOKS
to Grow In

*There are books to grow in
and books to know in,*

*Books that really please you
and books that sometimes tease you,*

*Books you're glad you found
and books you can't put down,*

*Books with funny pictures
and books that make you richer,*

*Books with a friendly tone—
books you want, all for your own!*

Up, Up, and Away!

DIRECTIONS: Open your *Write Away* handbook to page 3. Read about the five parts of *Write Away*. Fill in the missing words and color the balloons.

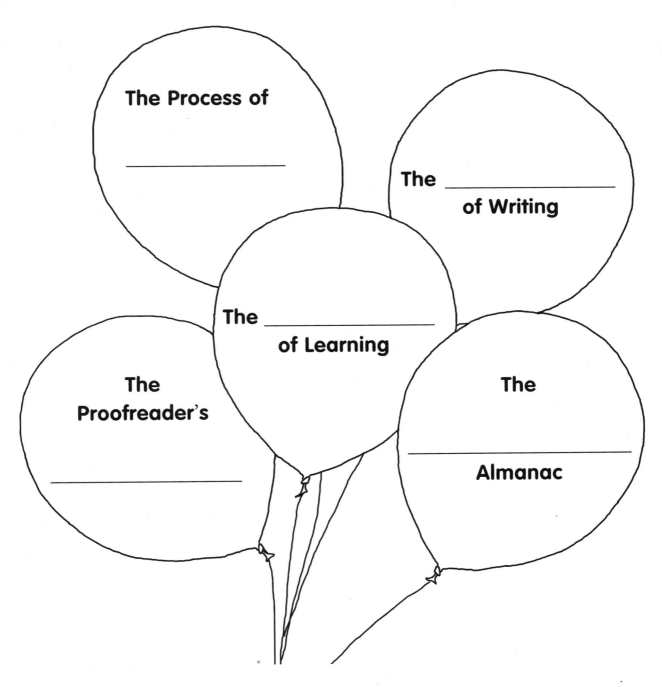

The Process of

_____

The _____

of Writing

The _____

of Learning

The
Proofreader's

_____

The

_____

Almanac

Getting to Know Your Handbook

DIRECTIONS: Find the table of contents in *Write Away*. Write down the beginning page number for each of these chapters.

Chapter Title	Page
1. Writing Friendly Letters	72
2. Using Theme Words	
3. Writing Sentences	
4. Telling Stories	
5. Making Shape Poems	
6. Making Posters	
7. Making Contractions	
8. Writing Add-On Stories	
9. Writing News Stories	
10. All About Maps	
11. Improving Handwriting	

DIRECTIONS: Take time to find these chapters in your book. Then double-check your page numbers.

Good Ideas About Writing

DIRECTIONS: On pages 13-19 in *Write Away,* you will find six children with good ideas about writing. On this page, connect each child with his or her idea. One has been done for you.

DOUGLAS

JENNA

BEN

1. Just keep writing, and have fun!

2. Write about subjects you really like.

3. To be a good writer, you have to practice.

4. Share your stories and poems.

5. Try different forms of writing.

6. Read a lot of different things.

LINDY

ROGER

KAYLA

Scavenger Hunt 1

1. Look at pages 20-21 in the handbook.
What is the first step in the writing process?

_____

2. Turn to page 43. How many publishing ideas are listed on
this page?

_____

3. Read page 73. What greeting did John use in his letter?

_____

4. Turn to page 112. Is a nonfiction book true or
make-believe?

_____

5. *Special Challenge:* Turn to the index in the back of the
handbook. On what page would you find "Name poetry"?

_____

Scavenger Hunt 2

1. Turn to page 179. Write two of the compound words listed on this page.

_____   _____

2. Turn to page 199. Find the example that will help you fill in these blanks.

_____ + _____ = triangle

3. Look at the contractions on page 203. What is the last contraction in the list?

_____

4. Read page 228. An oral report is part telling and part

_____ .

5. *Special Challenge:* Turn to the index in the back of the handbook. On what page would you find a "Venn diagram"?

_____

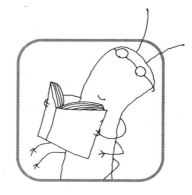

Scavenger Hunt 3

1. Read about underlining on page 253.
Underlining is used for titles of books and

_____ .

2. Find the words "dear" and "deer" on page 269. Circle the
word that names a type of animal.

dear   deer

3. Turn to page 294. A group of elephants is called a

_____ .

4. Page 321 shows handwriting tips. Write down the first tip
on the lines below.

_____

_____

5. *Special Challenge:* Turn to the index in the back of the
handbook. On what pages would you find out about "Maps"?

_____

Words in Write Away

DIRECTIONS: Fill in the blank boxes below with words from *Write Away*. Choose words from the chapters at the top of the chart. Each word should begin with the letter at the side of the chart. (Use the table of contents to find the chapters.)

	Using Theme Words	Checking Your Spelling	Using Phonics
w	windy		
r			
i			
t			time
e			

Answer Key

Write Away for You (page 12)
Decorate page

Up, Up, and Away! (page 13)
The Process of Writing
The Forms of Writing
The Tools of Learning
The Proofreader's Guide
The Student Almanac

Getting to Know Your Handbook (page 14)
1. p. 72
2. p. 284
3. p. 49
4. p. 224
5. p. 160
6. p. 106
7. p. 202
8. p. 134
9. p. 92
10. p. 300
11. p. 318

Good Ideas About Writing (page 15)
1. Kayla
2. Roger
3. Douglas
4. Ben
5. Jenna
6. Lindy

Scavenger Hunt 1 (page 16)
1. Plan   2. eight   3. Dear Grandma,   4. true   5. p. 167

Scavenger Hunt 2 (page 17)
1. football, backpack, and/or grasshopper   2. tri + angle = triangle
3. you've   4. showing   5. p. 234

Scavenger Hunt 3 (page 18)
1. magazines   2. deer   3. herd   4. Sit up straight when you write.   5. pp. 300-305

Words in Write Away (page 19)
Answers will vary.

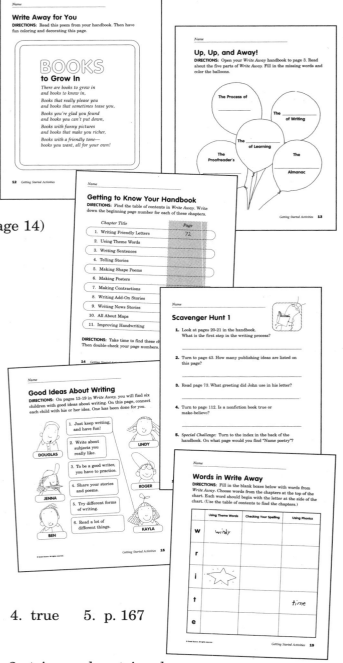

Using Write Away in the CLASSROOM

Teachers often ask how *Write Away* can be used in their classrooms. The answer to that question is easy. Teachers should think of *Write Away* as their teacher's aide, on hand to help students at all times—during class, throughout the school day, and later at home—with their writing, reading, and learning. The following pages provide ideas for making the handbook work in the classroom.

Where *Write Away* Fits In

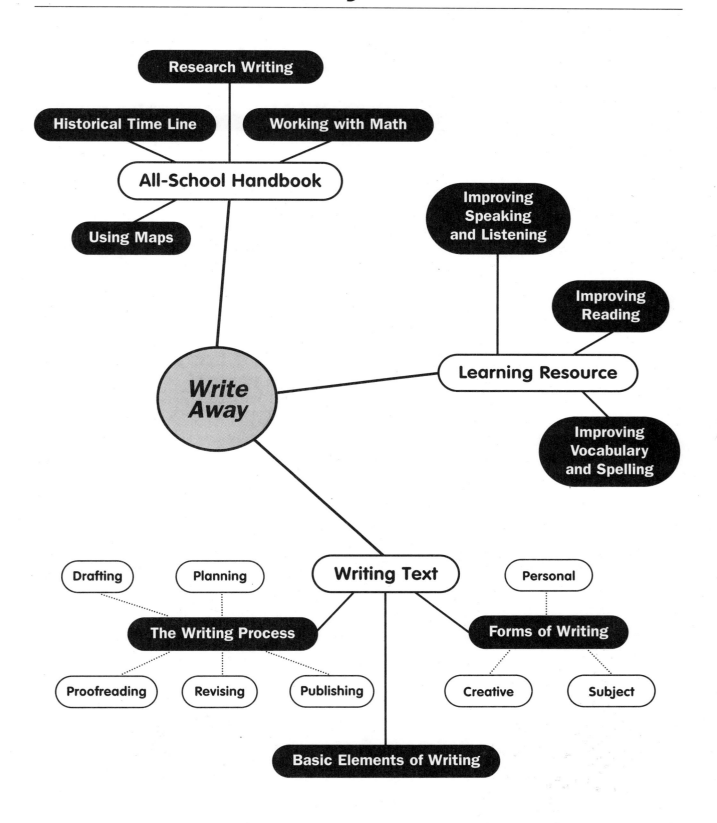

Research Writing

Historical Time Line

Working with Math

All-School Handbook

Using Maps

Improving Speaking and Listening

Improving Reading

Write Away

Learning Resource

Improving Vocabulary and Spelling

Drafting

Planning

Writing Text

Personal

The Writing Process

Forms of Writing

Proofreading

Revising

Publishing

Creative

Subject

Basic Elements of Writing

Framework of Writing Activities

The types of writing in *Write Away* are listed below in a possible framework or sequence of activities, moving from personal writing to writing that is more inventive and reflective. Teachers can use this framework as a starting point when planning a writing program with the handbook.

PERSONAL WRITING

Recording	**Keeping an Idea Notebook (p. 27)** **Writing in Journals (p. 65)** **Reading to Understand: Mapping (p. 184)**
Recalling and Remembering	**Writing Paragraphs: Sharing a Story (p. 60)** **Writing All-About-Me Stories (p. 76)**

SUBJECT WRITING

Introducing	**Learning to Interview (p. 214)**
Describing	**Writing Paragraphs: Describing Paragraphs (p. 57)**
Reporting	**Writing News Stories (p. 92)**
Corresponding	**Writing Friendly Notes (p. 68)** **Writing Friendly Letters (p. 72)** **Writing Business Letters (p. 96)**
Informing	**Writing Paragraphs: Giving Information (p. 59)** **Writing Directions (p. 102)** **Making Counting Books (p. 86)** **Making Posters (p. 106)**
Searching and Researching	**Writing Reports (p. 118)** **Making Picture Dictionaries (p. 126)**

CREATIVE WRITING

Imagining	**Writing Circle Stories (p. 131)** **Writing Add-On Stories (p. 134)** **Writing Fables (p. 138)** **Writing Mysteries (p. 144)**
Inventing	**Writing Small Poems (p. 151)** **Making Shape Poems (p. 160)** **Performing Stories (p. 218)**

REFLECTIVE WRITING

Persuading	**Writing Paragraphs: Giving Reasons (p. 61)**
Reviewing	**Writing About Books (p. 81)**

Yearlong Timetable

The next four pages provide a suggested yearlong timetable of writing activities using *Write Away*. Adjust the timetable to meet the needs of your students and the nature of your classroom.

Write Away Yearlong Timetable of Units — FIRST QUARTER

HB — *Write Away* Student Handbook
PG — *Language Series Program Guide* (Ring Binder)

Week	Writing Activities	Resources
1	**Introducing the Handbook**	HB, PG (Getting Started Activities)

Journal writing can be introduced at anytime and should be encouraged throughout the year.

Week	Writing Activities	Resources
2	**Starting to Write**	HB (pp. 13-19)
		PG (The Process of Writing, pp. 3-5)

Week	Writing Activities	Resources
3	**Writing Friendly Notes**	HB (pp. 68-71)
		PG (The Forms of Writing, pp. 7-11)

This form of writing encourages the use of classroom mailboxes.

Week	Writing Activities	Resources
4	**Making Picture Dictionaries**	HB (pp. 126-129)
	or	PG (The Forms of Writing, pp. 65-69)
	Making Counting Books	HB (pp. 86-91)
		PG (The Forms of Writing, pp. 27-30)

Both of these forms of writing are conducive to small-group or class books.

Week	Writing Activities	Resources
5	Continued from previous week.	

Week	Writing Activities	Resources
6	**Learning to Listen**	HB (pp. 212-213)
		PG (The Tools of Learning, pp. 47-51)

Week	Writing Activities	Resources
7	**Writing Directions**	HB (pp. 102-105)
		PG (The Forms of Writing, pp. 39-43)
	Writing Conferences	HB (pp. 38-39)
		PG (The Process of Writing, pp. 29-32)

Writing directions for someone who needs to read and understand them offers a natural opportunity for a writing conference.

Week	Writing Activities	Resources
8	Continued from previous week.	

Special Note: Use handbook chapters in "The Tools of Learning" and "The Proofreader's Guide" to enrich your students' writing and learning during the school year.

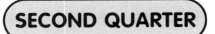
Week	Writing Activities	Resources
1	**Telling Stories**.	HB (pp. 224-227) PG (The Tools of Learning, pp. 63-65)
2	Continued from previous week.	
3	**Writing Sentences/ Writing Longer Sentences**.	HB (pp. 49-53) PG (The Process of Writing, pp. 41-47)

Learning about sentences is a vital, early step for young writers.

4	**Writing All-About-Me Stories**.	HB (pp. 76-79) PG (The Forms of Writing, pp. 17-21)
	Using the Writing Process	HB (pp. 20-25) PG (The Process of Writing, pp. 7-9)

Students are taught about the writing process within the context of personal narrative.

5	Continued from previous week.	
6	**Making Shape Poems**.	HB (pp. 160-165) PG (The Forms of Writing, pp. 97-102)
	More Poem Ideas	HB (pp. 166-167) PG (The Forms of Writing, p. 103)

These poetry activities could be centered around the winter holidays.

7	Continued from previous week.	
8	**Publishing Your Writing**.	HB (pp. 42-47) PG (The Process of Writing, pp. 37-39)

Apply the various modes of publishing to the different forms of writing done during the first two quarters of school.

Special Note: Use handbook chapters in "The Tools of Learning" and "The Proofreader's Guide" to enrich your students' writing and learning during the school year.

Week	Writing Activities	Resources
1	**Keeping an Idea Notebook**	HB (pp. 27-29)
		PG (The Process of Writing, pp. 11-14)
	Planning Your Writing	HB (pp. 30-31)
		PG (The Process of Writing, pp. 15-22)

Both of these chapters help children to understand the importance of prewriting activities.

2	**Writing Reports**	HB (pp. 118-125)
	or	PG (The Forms of Writing, pp. 57-64)
	Learning to Interview	HB (pp. 214-217)
		PG (The Tools of Learning, pp. 53-57)
	Revising Your Writing	HB (pp. 35-37)
		PG (The Process of Writing, pp. 25-27)

"Writing Reports" and "Learning to Interview" are research projects. Both activities offer young writers opportunities for writing and revising.

3	Continued from previous week.
4	Continued from previous week.

5	**Making Posters**	HB (pp. 106-109)
		PG (The Forms of Writing, pp. 45-49)
6	**Writing Friendly Letters**	HB (pp. 72-75)
		PG (The Forms of Writing, pp. 13-16)
7	**Writing Add-On-Stories**	HB (pp. 134-137)
	or	PG (The Forms of Writing, pp. 75-78)
	Writing Circle Stories	HB (pp. 131-133)
		PG (The Forms of Writing, pp. 71-74)

8	Continued from previous week.

Special Note: Use handbook chapters in "The Tools of Learning" and "The Proofreader's Guide" to enrich your students' writing and learning during the school year.

Week	Writing Activities	Resources
1	**Writing About Books**	HB (pp. 81-85)
		PG (The Forms of Writing, pp. 23-26)

Writing book reviews invites children to express their own opinions.

2	Continued from previous week.	

3	**Giving Oral Reports**	HB (pp. 228-229)
		PG (The Tools of Learning, pp. 67-70)

This activity allows children to share topics that they have recently learned about.

4	**Writing News Stories**	HB (pp. 92-95)
		PG (The Forms of Writing, pp. 31-34)

5	Continued from previous week.	

6	**Writing Fables**	HB (pp. 138-143)
	or	PG (The Forms of Writing, pp. 79-82)
	Writing Mysteries	HB (pp. 144-149)
		PG (The Forms of Writing, pp. 83-88)

7	Continued from previous week.	

8	**Performing Stories**	HB (pp. 218-223)
		PG (The Tools of Learning, pp. 59-61)

Performing stories is an enjoyable way to celebrate the literacy skills the children have acquired during this school year.

Special Note: Use handbook chapters in "The Tools of Learning" and "The Proofreader's Guide" to enrich your students' writing and learning during the school year.

The PROCESS of Writing

"The Process of Writing" section in *Write Away* contains everything your students need to know about writing—from a basic look at the steps in the writing process to a discussion of writing with computers, from guidelines for writing paragraphs to guidelines for combining sentences. Once your students become familiar with all of this information, they will turn to this section again and again whenever they have a question about their writing. The table of contents below lists the chapters in "The Process of Writing" section in the handbook. The page numbers refer to the location of each chapter summary in this guide.

Special Note: For minilessons related to the writing process, see pages 85-91.

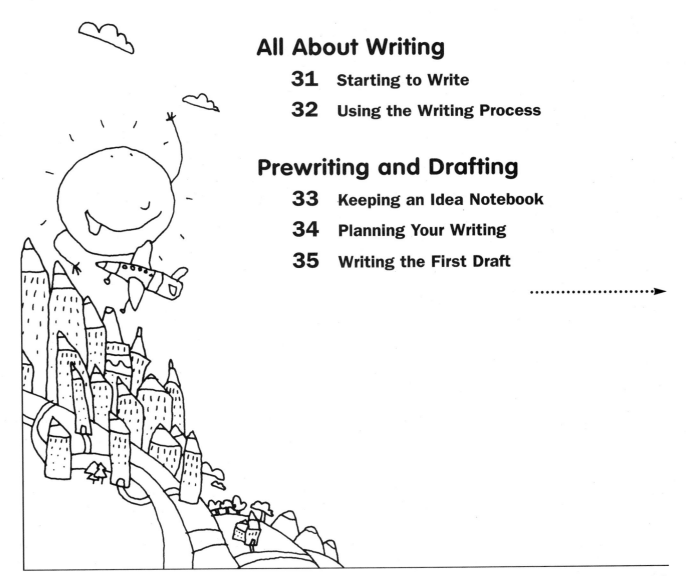

All About Writing

Prewriting and Drafting

Revising and Checking

Sentences and Paragraphs

Starting to Write

(handbook pages 13-19)

Classrooms where writing is celebrated are filled with notes, poems, journals, stories, plays, songs—fun! In these same classrooms, activities and materials are used to support the children's natural tendencies as language learners.

Starting to Write begins and ends with a key point about writing—it's fun! In this section of the handbook, six children share ideas to encourage young student writers—read, find interesting subjects, try different forms, practice, find an audience, and have fun.

Rationale

✔ **As writers, young students are at many different stages of development.**

✔ **Students need to begin building a source of writing ideas.**

✔ **Writing helps students to discover themselves—their strengths, what they like and don't like, etc.**

✔ **Writing is fun, especially when it is shared with others.**

Major Concepts

✳ **Writing is influenced by personal reading and experiences.** (pages 14-15)

✳ **There are many different forms of writing.** (page 16)

✳ **Practicing helps students to become better writers.** (page 17)

✳ **Writing is many different things, including a satisfying way to share and learn.** (pages 18-19)

Planning Notes

Materials: Student writing samples

Using the Writing Process

(handbook pages 20-25)

It's understandable that most children page through their books, reading, looking at the pictures, without really knowing how the books came to be! Young writers can learn about the stages of the writing process, becoming aware that writing is more than a simple pen-to-paper activity.

Using the Writing Process displays the five steps in the writing process. Then it goes on to show how Casey, a young writer, developed a story about her dog Muffy, following those steps in the process.

Rationale

✔ **Seeing the writing process in action helps students understand how it works.**

✔ **The writing process is a series of choices a writer makes as he or she shares ideas.**

Major Concepts

✳ **Prewriting involves different ways of planning.** (pages 20 and 22)

✳ **A first draft is a writer's first try at getting ideas down on paper.** (pages 20 and 23)

✳ **Revising means making changes to parts that don't work.** (pages 21 and 24)

✳ **Proofreading (checking) means checking for spelling, capital letters, and punctuation.** (pages 21 and 24)

Planning Notes

Materials: A favorite picture book

Keeping an Idea Notebook

(handbook pages 27-29)

An idea notebook is a place where writers collect their thoughts, snippets of information or conversations, questions, musings, and so on. Because writers keep notebooks, and jot in them on a regular basis, they are more aware of everything around them. Why not let children in on the secret?

In **Keeping an Idea Notebook,** we suggest that notebooks are "treasure chests." This discussion is followed by second-grade models and ways to use notebooks as starting points for writing.

Rationale

✔ **Students need a place for gathering seeds for writing.**

✔ **Keeping an idea notebook helps students become more aware of their world.**

Major Concepts

✱ An idea notebook is a place for students to keep thoughts for writing. (page 27)

✱ Ideas in notebooks can be used in different writing forms. (page 28)

✱ Ideas in notebooks can be used as writing prompts. (page 29)

Planning Notes

Materials: Small spiral notebooks, pencils, and books with main characters who keep notes about their lives

Here are two suggestions:

How to Get Famous in Brooklyn by Amy Hest
(Simon & Schuster 1995)

I'm in Charge of Celebrations by Byrd Baylor
(Charles Scribner's Sons 1986)

Reading/Writing Connections: Literature is filled with characters who live "wide-awake" lives, characters who, if they lived next door to us, would forever be caught writing in their idea notebooks. Ask students to talk about story characters they know who live "wide-awake" lives.

Planning Your Writing

(handbook pages 30-31)

Planning, often called prewriting, is the important first step in the writing process. Planning may include thinking, talking, writing, and drawing.

In **Planning Your Writing,** students are introduced to the three main parts of prewriting. The first two parts—thinking of subjects to write about and choosing the best one—are interdependent. The third part—collecting ideas—focuses on ways to find the details needed for a specific writing activity. The chapter includes a variety of collection ideas for children to use.

Rationale

✔ **Planning for writing involves thinking, making choices, and collecting ideas.**

✔ **It is important to collect ideas before writing.**

Major Concepts

✱ **Thinking about and choosing a topic for writing takes time and effort.** (page 30)

✱ **Some ways of collecting ideas are reading, talking, drawing, and writing.** (page 31)

Planning Notes

Materials: Paper, pencils, art materials

Early Literacy Connections: Planning for writing may be the most comfortable part of the writing process for some young learners. Gathering ideas, thinking them through, and talking about them may be the students' primary modes of communication for now. The importance of these activities for developing writers should not be underestimated. Some options for learners who are not yet able to write a first *or* final draft are dictating their information to a "scribe" (teacher or other adult), using a computer, or giving oral reports about the ideas they have collected.

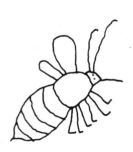

Writing the First Draft

(handbook pages 32-33)

Ask anybody, from a famous novelist to a second grader, "What's the hardest part of writing?" The answer will probably be, "Getting started." You can ease the way for your students by creating a writer-friendly classroom. Here are some ways to do it:

1. Provide an inviting environment with lots of interesting materials at the children's disposal. Have pencils, markers, crayons, various kinds of lined and unlined paper, chart paper, picture postcards, scissors, hole punchers, tape, and any other materials that will make writing interesting and enjoyable.

2. Present writing as a process instead of emphasizing the final product.

3. Offer students opportunities to make choices about their topics and forms of writing.

4. Encourage students to share and discuss their work with classmates.

5. Establish a writing-time routine, and have students write as often as possible.

6. Give assignments that involve writing for real audiences.

7. Read your own writing to students, inviting them to be a part of your writing process.

Writing the First Draft focuses on getting started. The chapter begins by explaining that writing the first draft simply means putting your ideas into sentences, and then putting sentences in the best order. It reassures students that they "can make changes later on." The next page offers several drafting tips.

Rationale

✔ **"Starting" is much easier when viewed as one step in the writing process.**

✔ **A first draft allows students to get their ideas down on paper without being overly concerned about mistakes.**

Major Concepts

✳ Writing a first draft means putting ideas into sentences. (page 32)

✳ It's important to plan how to begin. (page 33)

✳ A first draft is complete when all the ideas are on paper. (page 33)

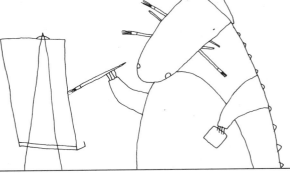

Revising Your Writing

(handbook pages 35-37)

Once a writer has a first draft, there's an opportunity to revise. Revising simply means making changes to improve the first draft.

Revising Your Writing opens with a quotation from a student writer who succinctly explains both the process and the result of revising: "My writing will be good if I make changes to parts I don't like." The next two pages explain how to go about making those changes. First there are five tips for revising, followed by reminders about and examples of a good beginning, middle, and ending.

Rationale

✔ **Revising is an important step in the writing process.**

✔ **When students learn to revise, they feel less intimidated by writing. They learn that they can change what they don't like.**

Major Concepts

✱ Revising means changing a piece of writing to make it better. (page 35)

✱ Young writers can practice revising techniques. (page 36)

✱ One important part of revising is making sure the writing has a good beginning, middle, and ending. (page 37)

Writing Conferences

(handbook pages 38-39)

Students often take part in informal writing conferences as they eagerly share their writing with classmates and teachers. And while most second graders cannot solve specific writing problems for each other, the sharing they do can still serve a purpose. The information in this chapter will help.

Writing Conferences begins by telling what a conference is and when it can help: when planning, when revising, and when checking. The following page explains the role of each partner in one kind of writing conference, a revising conference.

Rationale

✔ **Young writers love to share their work.**

✔ **Conferencing provides a structure and purpose for sharing.**

✔ **Conferencing helps students begin to evaluate writing.**

Major Concepts

✷ **In writing conferences, partners help each other plan and improve their writing.** (page 38)

✷ **In a revising conference, the partner talks about the writing while the writer listens and answers questions.** (page 39)

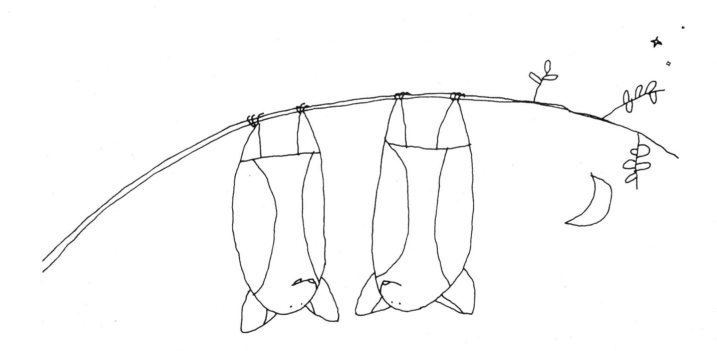

Checking for Errors

(handbook pages 40-41)

Students need to learn how to proofread their writing—to check their spelling, capitalization, and punctuation. Their primary purpose is to make their writing "reader friendly."

Checking for Errors begins by explaining that writing is not finished (ready to publish) until it has been checked for errors, or proofread. The next page gives three proofreading tips and a four-part proofreading checklist.

Rationale

✔ **Checking for errors is an important step in the writing process.**

✔ **Students gain a sense of accomplishment and pride when their work is error free.**

Major Concepts

✱ Writing is not finished until it has been proofread, or checked for errors. (page 40)

✱ Three steps in proofreading include reading the piece aloud, touching each word to check spelling, and finding a helper. (page 41)

✱ Students should check their writing for capitalization, end punctuation, and spelling. (page 41)

Publishing Your Writing

*(handbook
pages 42-47)*

Half the fun of any creative endeavor is sharing it with others. And that's exactly what publishing is all about. It is the natural culmination of the writing process. Of course, not every piece of writing gets published. For writing that is going to be shared with others, this step is always recommended.

Publishing Your Writing begins by explaining that *publishing* means sharing finished work. A list of eight publishing ideas follows. Next, two pages tell about drawing pictures to illustrate writing. The chapter's final two pages tell how to make a book.

Rationale

✔ **Publishing is the culmination of the writing process.**

✔ **Publishing increases interest in writing and builds confidence in the writer.**

✔ **Publishing motivates student writers to do their best at each stage of the writing process.**

Major Concepts

✱ **Publishing means sharing finished writing. (page 42)**

✱ **There are many ways to publish writing. (page 43)**

✱ **Sometimes writers add pictures before they publish. (pages 44-45)**

✱ **Writers may publish their writing in book form. (pages 46-47)**

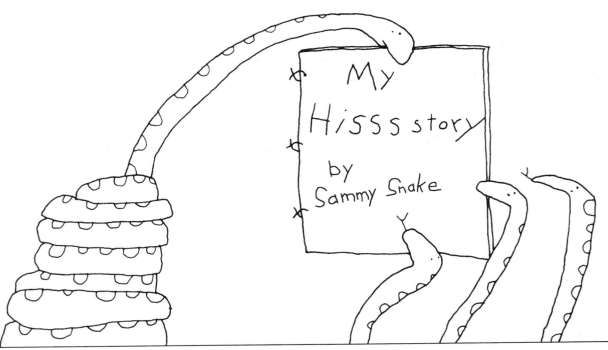

Writing Sentences/ Writing Longer Sentences

(handbook pages 49-53)

For young learners, an understanding of sentences is important in their development as writers. Writing is, after all, making statements, asking questions, giving commands, and so on. Certainly, as young learners read and write and speak during the primary grades, their sentence sense will naturally develop. However, teachers can also promote sentence awareness in specific language activities.

Writing Sentences provides an excellent starting point for direct instruction related to sentences. The opening page addresses the concept of sentence completeness (what a sentence is). The next page introduces students to the terms *subject* and *verb*. The last page discusses subject/verb agreement and a common sentence problem, stringing ideas together with the words "and then."

Writing Longer Sentences explains that writers can combine short sentences to make longer ones. The chapter shows three ways to do this: combine subjects, combine verbs, and combine other words.

Rationale

✔ **A sentence is the basic unit of communication.**

✔ **We use sentences continually—in our writing, reading, and speaking.**

✔ **Learning to write longer sentences improves fluency.**

✔ **Writing becomes more enjoyable as students learn to express themselves in sentences of various lengths and styles.**

Major Concepts

✱ A sentence, a group of words that tells a complete idea, has a naming part (subject) and a telling part (verb). (pages 49-50)

✱ Subjects and verbs must agree in number. (page 51)

✱ Young writers should avoid stringing together too many ideas with *and then's*. (page 51)

✱ Young writers can combine short sentences to make longer ones. (pages 52-53)

Planning Notes

Materials: Paper, pencils

Chapter Link: "Checking Your Sentences," pages 274-275.

Writing Paragraphs

(handbook pages 54-61)

When students are learning about paragraphs, they are learning to organize their thoughts. The paragraph provides one structure for sharing whatever they have on their minds, whether it's a serious explanation or a funny story.

Writing Paragraphs begins by telling students that they can use a paragraph to describe, give information, share a story, or give reasons. The next page offers a definition and explains the three parts of every paragraph. On the following page, students can read through a model with the three parts labeled. Next, students are walked through the process of writing a describing paragraph. The chapter ends with three more student models, one giving information, another sharing a story, and one giving reasons.

Rationale

✔ **Understanding paragraph structure helps students organize their thoughts when writing explanations, descriptions, narratives, and more.**

✔ **The paragraph is the basic unit of longer compositions, so learning to write one is a step toward writing stories, essays, letters, etc.**

✔ **Understanding what makes a good paragraph will help students as they revise their writing.**

Major Concepts

✳ Every paragraph has a beginning, a middle, and an ending. (page 55)

✳ Writing paragraphs involves four steps: planning, writing, revising, and checking. (pages 57-58)

✳ A paragraph can share a story. (page 60)

✳ A paragraph can give reasons. (page 61)

Planning Notes

Materials: A selection of the four types of paragraphs from students' favorite books, textbooks, the handbook, newspapers, magazines, etc.

The FORMS of Writing

You can build a timely and comprehensive writing program around "The Forms of Writing" section in *Write Away*. Included in this section of the handbook are guidelines for writing journals, book reviews, business letters, poems, mysteries, and much more.

"The Forms of Writing" section of this guide coordinates with the chapters in the handbook. You will find easy-to-follow chapter notes helpful for program planning.

Special Note: For minilessons related to the forms of writing, see pages 92-99.

Personal Writing

Subject Writing

Research Writing

Story Writing

Poetry Writing

Writing in Journals

(handbook pages 65-67)

In the introduction to *The Journal Book,* Toby Fulwiler says, "Human beings find meaning in the world by exploring it through language—through their own easy talky language." Examples of such language can be found in many places—from talk in the school lunchroom to the informal language found in classroom journals.

Writing in Journals begins with a simple, straightforward explanation: Journals are a good place to "write about how you feel and what you think." This introduction is followed by a list of journal-writing tips in which students are encouraged, among other things, to reread their journals often. The chapter includes three journal entries written by a second grader.

Rationale

✔ **Students find meaning through informal language, both spoken and written.**

✔ **Informal journal writing gives students room to think.**

✔ **Journal writing encourages many types of thinking—from simple observation and recall to question-formation, analysis, and synthesis.**

Major Concepts

✱ Journals are places to write about what you feel and think. (page 65)

✱ Journal writing can remain informal. (page 66)

✱ Students should write in their journals frequently and reread their entries often. (page 66)

✱ Students can write about and react to their lives and to what they are learning and reading. (pages 66-67)

Planning Notes

Materials: Notebooks or composition books, pencils, a variety of crayons and markers

Early Literacy Connections: When writing in journals, young writers may be encouraged to invent spellings for words they don't know how to spell. They can record their ideas with ease, as well as use their evolving ideas about sound/symbol relationships. Also, the "invented spellings" can be used as clues for determining the developmental spelling levels of your students. This information will help you plan appropriate spelling instruction.

Writing Friendly Notes

(handbook pages 68-71)

Writing Friendly Notes encourages students to write notes to many people in their lives—for different reasons and in a variety of ways. The introduction lists possible audiences and mentions the special attraction of friendly notes. Models illustrate four reasons for writing notes: to tell something you know, to send good wishes, to say thank you, and to share a message. Finally, this chapter offers ideas for adding special touches to friendly notes.

Rationale

✔ **Writing friendly notes is an easy way for children to send a message to another person.**

✔ **Friendly notes encourage ongoing writing practice.**

Major Concepts

✱ People like to get friendly notes. It tells them that the writer cares about them. (page 68)

✱ People write friendly notes for a variety of reasons. (pages 69-70)

Planning Notes

Materials: Stationery, small notepaper, construction paper, colored pencils, pens, rubber stamps, stickers (You may choose to set up a communication station in your classroom.)

Technology Connections: Your students may be able to send friendly E-mail messages. Perhaps you can make a connection with a class in another state.

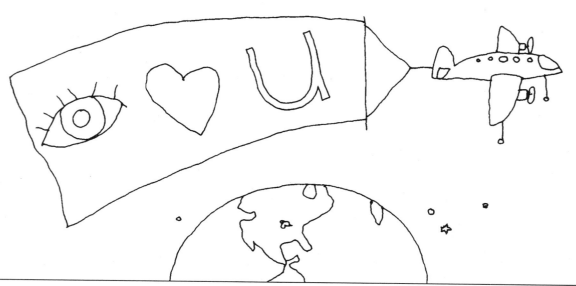

Writing Friendly Letters

(handbook pages 72-75)

Friendly letters offer a way for students to reach out to friends and family through writing. And for all their efforts, young writers can enjoy the letters they receive from a responsive audience.

Writing Friendly Letters begins by explaining that friendly letters are similar to friendly notes—except that friendly letters travel. A student model shows the five parts of a friendly letter: date, greeting, body, closing, and signature. Then the four steps of writing a friendly letter are outlined, and the chapter concludes with a hint about sending letters.

Rationale

✔ **Writing friendly letters is an important social skill.**

✔ **Friendly letters communicate news and express thanks.**

Major Concepts

✱ **Friendly letters can reach friends and relatives faraway.** (page 72)

✱ **There are five parts to a friendly letter: date, greeting, body, closing, and signature.** (page 73)

Planning Notes

Materials: Different sizes and colors of paper and envelopes for stationery, colored pencils, pens, rubber stamps, stickers

Reading/Writing Connections: *The Jolly Postman* by Janet and Allan Ahlberg (Little, Brown 1986) provides examples of friendly letters in action. *Don't Forget to Write* by Martina Selway (Ideals 1992) also includes friendly letters.

School and Community Uses: Students might write thank-you notes after a memorable field trip or assembly. Also encourage your young "reporters" to write friendly letters to the school newsletter editor, sharing your classroom news.

Technology Connections: Many children's word-processing programs have "print shop" features that are a natural match for friendly letters. Explore your options and take time to teach your class how to type their friendly letters on the computer. Often, they will have choices of fonts, pictures, and borders to personalize their letters.

Writing All-About-Me Stories

(handbook pages 76-79)

Telling stories about themselves helps young writers see that good stories come from one's own experience. It demonstrates that a writer's most important resource is his or her own life.

The introduction points to the great variety possible in **Writing All-About-Me Stories**. Next there is a student model, followed by suggestions to help students find personal events to write about, as well as a tip for telling the story aloud before starting to write it down. Guidelines for writing, revising, and checking follow.

Rationale

✔ **Everyone has a story to tell.**

✔ **All-about-me stories provide students with countless writing topics.**

✔ **Writing a story begins with wanting to tell a story.**

Major Concepts

✱ **An all-about-me story tells something that happened to the writer.** (page 76)

✱ **Students can use the writing process to write an all-about-me story.** (pages 78-79)

✱ **Students can enrich their stories with a strong opening.** (page 79)

Planning Notes

Materials: Paper, pencils, art materials, a collection of first-person picture books

Reading/Writing Connections: Look for picture books that center on themes common to second-grade interests, such as James Stevenson's childhood reminiscences in *When I Was Nine, Higher on the Door, July,* and *Fun/No Fun* (all published by Greenwillow). Choose and share one scene that will elicit student storytelling. For example, after hearing such stories as *Thunder Cake* by Patricia Pollaco (Philomel 1990) and *Rumble, Thumble, Boom!* by Anna Grossnickle Hines (Greenwillow 1992), every second grader will have a follow-up thunderstorm story.

School and Community Uses: Invite students to write stories about incidents from their kindergarten days, and then have them read their stories to present-day kindergartners.

Ask students to write stories about things they've done with a grandparent or other older person. Have them share their stories on a class visit to a senior citizens residence.

Writing About Books

(handbook pages 81-85)

Kids enjoy talking about the books they love. And they can learn how to turn these natural testimonials into simple book reviews.

Writing About Books opens by linking the fun of reading a good book with the fun of sharing it. There are two student model reviews of books: one of fiction and one of a nonfiction. These reviews are followed by guidelines for writing a basic book review.

Rationale

✔ **Writing book reviews allows children to share their ideas.**

✔ **Writing book reviews helps students think about what they read.**

Major Concepts

✱ **Writing book reviews provides an opportunity to share ideas.** (page 81)

✱ **Model reviews answer two questions: What is this book about? Why do I like this book?** (pages 82-83)

✱ **A book review requires planning (choosing a book, thinking about it) and writing (answering the two main questions).** (page 84)

Planning Notes

Materials: Writing supplies, book jacket testimonial blurbs that answer either of the book review questions

Reading/Writing Connections: Have students keep simple reading logs. After every silent or buddy reading session, students record the title and author of the book they are reading, noting whether the book is "true" or "make-believe." Then students write one sentence about what they have read. If students are partway through a book, they may begin, "I like the part about . . . " When students finish a book, they should write two sentences:

"This book is about . . . "
"I like this book because . . . "

School and Community Uses: Reading logs make useful monthly reports to parents. The report also shows parents their child's reading preferences.

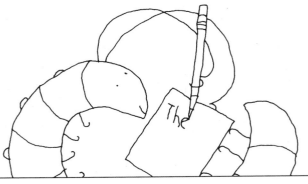

Making Counting Books

(handbook pages 86-91)

Children enjoy mastering patterns. Because number patterns can be simple or complex, students of all abilities can find satisfaction in creating their own counting books.

Making Counting Books begins with a familiar counting jingle, "One, two, buckle my shoe," reminding children that they already know the format of a counting book. Then the chapter provides two pages of a student model counting book, along with some explanation. This is followed by a plan to help students find a number pattern, pick a subject, and create their own books. Finally, a sampling from another student book using numbers and rhyme is shared.

Rationale

✔ **Young children enjoy creating their own books.**

✔ **Using number patterns helps students strengthen pattern awareness, critical to the development of mathematical skills.**

✔ **Reading classmates' counting books helps students discover new number patterns.**

✔ **Writing counting books supports the math-writing connection.**

Major Concepts

✱ **Besides numbers counting books need special words and pictures. (page 86)**

✱ **Students can pick interesting subjects and then use words that have the same initial sounds or words that rhyme to make their books fun to read. (pages 87, 88, 91)**

✱ **There are many number patterns to choose from when writing a counting book. (pages 87, 89, 90)**

Planning Notes

Materials: Paper, pencils, art supplies, collections of counting books

Reading/Writing Connections: Counting books are available in libraries. Some good models include *One Gorilla* by Atsuko Morozumi (Farrar 1990), *One Bear with Bees in His Hair* by Jakki Wood (Dutton 1990), and *The 12 Circus Rings* by Seymour Chwast (Harcourt 1993).

Writing News Stories

(handbook pages 92-95)

News stories about school activities provide second graders with viable writing experiences that go beyond the personal narrative.

Writing News Stories begins by talking about news writing as a sharing process. A model news story is provided, and each part is labeled and defined. Students are then taken through the process of writing a news story, including planning, writing, revising, and checking.

Rationale

✔ **As students see adults reading newspapers, they become aware that this is an important form of writing.**

✔ **Writing news stories helps students see the importance of organization.**

Major Concepts

✱ Writing news stories involves sharing information with readers. (page 92)

✱ A news story has a specific structure. (pages 93)

✱ Information for news stories comes from a variety of sources. (page 94)

✱ News writers need to follow the news-story format. (page 95)

Planning Notes

Materials: Notebooks, pencils

Technology Connections: If possible, have students read the news headlines via an Internet provider every day for a week. Even though they may not understand the events, reading headlines provides the following realizations for students:

> news changes daily
>
> news writers fit a lot of information into a headline

Reading/Writing Connections: Bring a newspaper to class and find an appropriate story to read each day.

Deadline!: From News to Newspaper by Gail Gibbons (Harper 1987) gives primary students an inside look at a small-town newspaper.

Writing Business Letters

(handbook pages 96-101)

Learning how to write business letters at an early age gives students a new confidence. They find they can send for information, order things, and even try to solve problems for themselves.

Writing Business Letters begins by explaining how grown-ups use business letters all the time. The chapter encourages students to write business letters, too, offering seven tips for the process. Then the six parts of a business letter are defined and labeled in a student model: heading, inside address, salutation, body, closing, and signature. The chapter concludes with information about addressing the envelope and sending the letter.

Rationale

✔ **Writing business letters is a useful life skill.**

✔ **The business-letter form emphasizes clear, specific communication— an important skill for young learners.**

Major Concepts

✱ Business letters can be used to send for information, to order things, or to try to solve problems. (page 96)

✱ There is a specific format for business letters. (pages 97-99)

✱ There are six parts to a business letter: heading, inside address, salutation, body, closing, and signature. (pages 98-99)

✱ There are standard requirements for sending a business letter. (pages 100-101)

Planning Notes

Materials: Pencils (pens), paper, sample letters

Reading/Writing Connections: *Free Stuff for Kids* by the Free Stuff Editors (1995), director Bruce Lansky, has a wealth of sources that will send things to kids, just for the asking.

School and Community Uses: Students can use business letters to communicate with other members of their community and beyond. They can write invitations to guest speakers. They can write for information about a subject they are studying or, if there is a particular local issue that troubles your class, they can write business letters to try to solve the problem.

Writing Directions

(handbook pages 102-105)

Writing directions is an enjoyable way for students to share their expertise with others. Second graders revel in their growing abilities, and this form of writing is an excellent way for them to show what they know.

Writing Directions begins by noting that everyone is good at something, and that students can write directions to explain how their skill is done. Another use for writing directions is to explain how to get to a special place. Two student models are given. The chapter concludes with a four-step process for writing a set of directions.

Rationale

✔ **Writing is a useful tool for sharing step-by-step information.**

✔ **Learning how to order steps in a process is a valuable skill.**

Major Concepts

* **Writing directions is useful for explaining how to do a particular skill.** (page 102)

* **Writing directions is also useful for explaining how to get to a special place.** (page 102)

* **Time words, like *first* and *then*, or numbered steps will make directions clear and easy to follow.** (page 104)

Planning Notes

Materials: Kids' cookbooks, magazines and books that include science experiments

Across-the-Curriculum Possibilities: Students can use their skills to write directions for getting to different parts of the school or to community landmarks. They may also explain what happens in various scientific processes (how a seed grows, how a caterpillar turns into a butterfly).

School and Community Uses: Your students can provide visitors with clear directions on how to get to different parts of your school building. They could also publish a how-to book filled with their expertise on different processes and skills and contribute it to the media center.

Making Posters

(handbook pages 106-109)

At first glance, poster making may appear to be a simple cut-and-paste exercise. However, creating posters is not just a fun activity students can succeed at. It also introduces them to a valuable skill they'll find useful in many situations. Students can use the same organizational plan they use for posters when they need to add graphics to reports. The tips offered in this chapter will help children convey any message more clearly and effectively.

Making Posters begins by comparing making a poster to writing a big note—whether it announces an event or simply states facts. There are two model posters, and the chapter concludes with tips to help students make their own posters.

Rationale

✔ **Poster making develops basic organizational skills.**

✔ **Posters require precise language and attention to detail.**

✔ **Making posters helps students integrate visual and written information.**

Major Concepts

✱ Posters can announce events or share ideas. (pages 106-108)

✱ Posters require careful planning to use pictures and words together effectively. (page 109)

Planning Notes

Materials: Actual posters from the school or community, poster-making supplies (paper for sketching ideas, poster board or large pieces of paper, scissors, paste, glue, tape, pencils, crayons, markers, etc.)

Technology Connections: Your students may be able to create posters using computer programs. The most available resource will probably be a word-processing program with a "print shop" feature.

School and Community Uses: Ask if there is an upcoming school event that needs publicity. Your class could design several different posters to promote the event.

Across-the-Curriculum Possibilities: Ask students to create posters to share information they are learning in science, social studies, or math class.

Using the Library

(handbook pages 111-117)

Libraries are treasuries of facts and details, stories, music, and more. Typical resources include newspapers, videos, artwork, globes, tapes, and computer software. A good library and its staff will always be a student's best source of information.

Using the Library opens by explaining to children that a library is a place to find many kinds of books. In general, this chapter gives students a foundation on which to build their library skills. The four kinds of books—fiction, nonfiction, biography, and reference—are defined, along with information on where to find them on the shelves. Introductory lessons on using the card catalog, a computer catalog, and on understanding call numbers are also provided. Finally, the parts of nonfiction books are explained, including the table of contents and the index.

Rationale

✔ **Students need to understand that different kinds of books serve different purposes.**

✔ **Students need to learn how to find books in a library.**

Major Concepts

＊ **There are different kinds of books in a library, each kind in its own place.** (pages 112-113)

＊ **The card or computer catalog tells about all the books in the library.** (pages 114-115)

＊ **Nonfiction books are shelved by their call numbers.** (page 116)

＊ **Students will get more out of nonfiction books when they understand their parts.** (page 117)

Planning Notes

Materials: A selection of fiction, nonfiction, biography, and reference books, a few catalog cards (author, subject, and title) and the books they refer to, computer catalog printouts of some entries

Writing Reports

(handbook pages 118-125)

Classrooms where children are searching for information and reporting their findings are very exciting places. When they have the opportunity to choose topics of interest, do research, and then record what they have learned, children are onto something new and wonderful.

Writing Reports begins with an introduction about a boy intent on studying his favorite dinosaur. Young writers are then guided through an information search; helpful organizing ideas—note cards and gathering grids; instruction in writing the report; and a student model. The chapter ends with a list of alternatives to the traditional report format, and includes a model poem and story.

Rationale

✔ **Students need the opportunity to explore topics of interest.**

✔ **Children build research skills and begin to think critically as they select, organize, and share material in a written report.**

Major Concepts

✳ **Selecting an interesting topic and asking questions about it is the first step in report writing. (pages 118-119)**

✳ **Note cards and gathering grids help students record and organize information. (pages 120-121)**

✳ **Reports have a beginning, a middle, and an ending—name the subject, share information, and give a brief review or personal response. (page 122)**

✳ **Pictures add meaning to reports. (page 123)**

✳ **There are many ways to report on information. (pages 124-125)**

Planning Notes

Materials: Books and other resources about topics you are studying, time for library trips, large paper for grids, note cards, a large wall chart

Making Picture Dictionaries

*(handbook
pages 126-129)*

Picture dictionaries offer an enjoyable introduction to the world of words and their meanings. Their ABC order make them easy to use, and pictures add interest and enhance meaning.

Making Picture Dictionaries begins by explaining a few simple characteristics of this writing form—entries in ABC order, some important words about each entry, and, of course, pictures! Example pages from a student model are followed by tips that children can use to write their own dictionaries.

Rationale

✔ **Children are used to seeing information presented in visual form, so they will welcome the chance to write and draw about subjects of interest.**

✔ **Picture dictionaries provide a familiar structure for arranging and organizing information.**

✔ **Writing picture dictionaries helps children separate fact from fiction.**

Major Concepts

✱ **Picture dictionaries are in ABC order and use words and drawings to convey information.** (pages 126-128)

✱ **Each word-page should be about the subject.** (page 129)

✱ **Each page in the dictionary should contain a picture and facts.** (page 129)

Planning Notes

Materials: A variety of supplies for writing and drawing, a collection of picture dictionaries and ABC books

Technology Connections: *Kid Art*™ offers a curriculum collection of graphics to be used with *Kid Pix* and *Kid Pix Studio* computer drawing programs (Brøderbund, 1-800-474-8840). Using *Kid Pix Studio,* young students can create technology-based picture dictionaries that include sound.

School and Community Uses: Other primary-grade students will enjoy reading your students' picture dictionaries. An A-to-Z hallway display of sample pages, at least one from each student's book, is a nice way to publish student work.

Writing Circle Stories

(handbook pages 131-133)

Circle stories begin and end in the same place. There are all types. Some have a realistic tone, while others are fantastic flights of fancy in which the main character leaves home, enters the big wide world, and returns by story's end.

Writing Circle Stories begins with a simple definition of the genre and then tells about Jane, a second grader who loves to read and write this type of tale. Jane has read *If You Give a Mouse a Cookie* by Laura Joffe Numeroff, and after drawing a story map, writes "If You Give a Kitten Some String!" Jane's story is followed by a few story-writing tips.

Rationale

✔ **The patterns in circle stories are satisfying and comforting to young children.**

✔ **Circle stories provide students with a structure they can easily understand and use.**

✔ **The prediction process in circle stories engages readers across all skill and developmental levels.**

Major Concepts

✱ A circle story begins and ends in the same place. (page 131)

✱ Children can get ideas for their own circle stories from stories they read and hear. (page 131)

✱ Before writing, students may draw pictures or a story map representing their plot line. (pages 132-133)

✱ Reading many circle stories will help students write their own. (page 133)

Planning Notes

Materials: Sample circle stories, including *If You Give a Mouse a Cookie*, chart paper, pencils, paper, crayons

Reading/Writing Connections: The handbook suggests that students read several circle stories before trying to write one. For title suggestions, see the "Reading/Writing Connection" section of this guide.

Writing Add-On Stories

(handbook pages 134-137)

Add-on stories are pleasing for children to read and write. They are immediately engaged by the repetition in this story form, and are also delighted to anticipate a surprise ending.

Writing Add-On Stories focuses on "Dance Steps," a story about a girl who is on a quest to learn how to tap-dance. With example planning notes from the model story, young writers are guided through the steps of writing their own add-on stories.

Rationale

✔ **Add-on tales involve simple plots and lots of repetition, appealing to young readers.**

✔ **The predictable add-on story is a nonthreatening form for young readers.**

Major Concepts

✳ **Add-on stories are fun to read and fun to write.** (pages 134-135)

✳ **Students can write an add-on story following a simple process.** (pages 136-137)

✳ **Add-on stories involve problem solving and surprise endings.** (page 137)

Planning Notes

Materials: Paper, pencils, crayons and markers, a variety of add-on tales

Reading/Writing Connections: Reading stories like *Is Your Mama a Llama?* by Deborah Guarino (Scholastic 1989), *A Guest Is a Guest* by John Himmelman (Dutton 1991), and *The Napping House* by Audrey Wood (Harcourt 1984) will acquaint students with the add-on pattern.

Early Literacy Connections: The repetition in add-on stories gives students an opportunity to develop fluency in their reading and writing. You may want to point out the words and phrases that are repeated in each story. For example, the phrase "sorry, I only know how to . . ." is repeated three times in "Dance Steps." And in *The Napping House*, the phrase "where everyone is sleeping" comes up again and again.

Writing Fables

*(handbook
pages 138-143)*

Never cry wolf. Slow but steady wins the race. In many languages around the world, familiar phrases like these have been entertaining and instructing us for more than 2,500 years. They are the morals, or lessons, that we learn from stories called fables. (Abraham Lincoln knew Aesop's fables by heart, and used them many times to explain his actions to others.)

Writing Fables begins with a clear definition: "A fable is a story that teaches a lesson." An example lesson is given—"slow but steady wins the race," the well-known moral from "The Tortoise and the Hare." After this introduction, students may read another fable, "The Wolf and the Kid," which is followed by four steps that take them through the fable-writing process. To help children get started, there are lists of possible characters and lessons, which are intended to provide food for thought.

Rationale

✔ **Fables show that we can learn from reading and thinking about what characters do and say.**

✔ **Fables are clear, simple stories that can help children understand story structure.**

✔ **Fables invite illustration and dramatization—perfect second-grade fare.**

Major Concepts

✳ A fable is a story that teaches a lesson. (pages 138 and 142)

✳ Fable characters are usually animals. (pages 140-141)

✳ Fable characters face a problem or need to learn a lesson. (page 142)

Planning Notes

Materials: Copies of many fables; drawing, painting, and writing materials

Early Literacy Connections: To improve children's comprehension, and thereby broaden their vocabularies, have them sketch a scene from one of the fables you read aloud—or from one of the student's fables. These simple stories are fun to illustrate. Often there are only a few characters, the action is concentrated, and the detail is concrete.

Technology Connections: *Living Books: Volume I* (stories on CD-ROM), produced by Brøderbund (1-800-474-8840), includes "The Tortoise and the Hare: Aesop's Fable."

Writing Mysteries

(handbook pages 144-149)

Young readers like looking for clues in their reading. They enjoy solving simple mysteries. For some students, writing their own mysteries may prove challenging. However, following the guidelines laid down for them will surely bring some reward, if only the fun of dreaming up their own mystery plots.

Writing Mysteries begins with this advice: "Follow the clues." The students read Josh's story, "The Case of the Missing Ring." The final three pages offer four steps to follow when writing a mystery.

Rationale

✔ **The excitement and suspense of mystery stories appeal to young readers and writers.**

✔ **Mysteries invite students to make predictions.**

✔ **Reading and writing mysteries can improve reading skills, as children choose to take more time to comprehend and enjoy this story form.**

✔ **Mysteries help students refine their powers of observation.**

Major Concepts

✱ Students like to read and write mysteries. (pages 144-146)

✱ A mystery story has a problem that needs to be solved. (page 147)

✱ Writers must introduce their main character and tell about the problem early in the story. (page 148)

✱ Readers need clues. (pages 148-149)

✱ A mystery needs a satisfying ending. (pages 148-149)

Planning Notes

Materials: Paper and pencils, mystery stories, a "picture mystery"

Technology Connections: For Macintosh™ and Windows™, "Living Words Frameworks" (from Brøderbund) offers a mystery for young readers on CD-ROM, *Harry and the Haunted House.* Brøderbund also has a junior-detective edition of *Carmen Sandiego* (PreK-3).

Writing Small Poems

(handbook pages 151-159)

Small poems are short poems about everyday things—perfect fare for young writers. Capturing sights, sounds, and feelings from their own experiences rewards young poets in what may be their first attempts at crafting their language. The power of strong descriptions and the surprises of unusual comparisons can introduce young writers to a lifelong adventure—poetry.

Writing Small Poems begins with a 27-word model, "The Pool," by Clay, a second grader. Many readers can relate to Clay's first line, "I live at the pool in the summer"; it illustrates the chapter's opening remark: "Writing a small poem is a fun way to tell about everyday things." After reading another model, students are encouraged to make friends with small poems. They are also given guidelines for writing their own poems.

Rationale

✔ **Writing small poems gives young writers a chance to talk and write about the everyday things they care about.**

✔ **Writing small poems helps children focus on exact language.**

Major Concepts

✱ Small poems are about everyday things and use few words. (page 151)

✱ It is good practice to read and share poetry, and to record favorite poems. Poetry writers read poetry and often record their favorite poems. (page 153)

✱ Students can use lists to gather ideas for poems. (page 154)

✱ Poetry uses strong action words and makes comparisons. (pages 155 and 159)

✱ Attention is paid to making pleasing sounds in poetry. (pages 155 and 158)

Planning Notes

Materials: A collection or two of small poems (for example, *all the small poems* by Valerie Worth/Farrar 1987 or *Sing to the Sun* by Bryan Ashley/HarperCollins 1992), paper and pencils

Making Shape Poems

(handbook pages 160-167)

Young writers love the language play of shape poems. In a shape poem, the arrangement of the letters and words on the page adds meaning to the poem. Poems can take the shape of a skyscraper, a swan, waves, a tornado—anything the writer imagines.

Making Shape Poems begins with a poem by J. Patrick Lewis, the author of *Doodle Dandies* (Anne Schwartz Books, scheduled for a 1998 publishing date). Following Lewis' poem are two student models, one demonstrating a filled shape, the other an outlined one. Next, students learn how to write shape poems. The chapter ends with four more word-play poetry ideas.

Rationale

✔ **Young children enjoy reading and writing shape poems.**

✔ **Shape and word-play poems encourage creative thinking.**

✔ **Fun poetic forms support reading/spelling connections.**

Major Concepts

✱ Shape poems are fun to write and draw. (page 160)

✱ Students can pour words into shapes or make shapes with words. (pages 161-162)

✱ Students work to fit words and shapes together. (pages 163-165)

✱ There are many ways to play with words through poetry. (pages 166-167)

Planning Notes

Materials: Paper, pencils, art supplies, collections of poetry including shape poems, pictures or cutouts of various shapes

Technology Connections: Children will enjoy creating interesting shape poems with *Kid Pix Studio* (1996), a favorite computer drawing program. Also, teachers familiar with the World Wide Web might create a home page filled with shape poems! See *The World Wide Web for Teachers* by Bard Williams (IDG Books Worldwide 1996).

School and Community Uses: Your students can partner with younger students to write poems about favorite shapes.

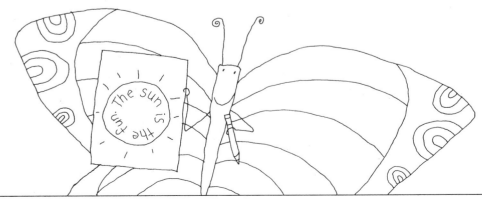

The TOOLS of Learning

"The Tools of Learning" will help students improve all of their study and learning skills. Included in this section of the handbook are chapters on reading, vocabulary, speaking, working in groups, test taking, and much more. There are even guidelines for reading graphics and performing stories. The table of contents below lists all of the chapters in "The Tools of Learning" section in the handbook. The page numbers refer to the location of each chapter summary in this guide.

Special Note: For minilessons related to the tools of learning, see pages 100-104.

Reading Skills

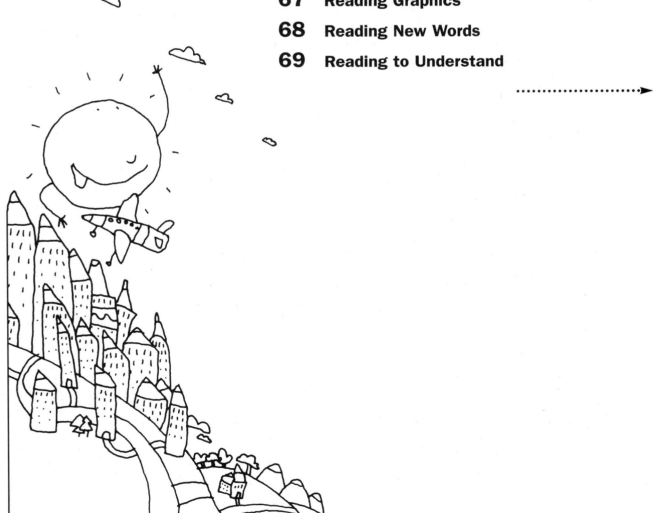

Working with Words

Speaking and Listening Skills

Learning Skills

Reading Graphics

(handbook pages 171-175)

Children are surrounded by information conveyed through words, symbols, and pictures. Textbooks, magazines, newspapers, brochures, billboards, and signs present information in both words and graphics. Some signs use graphics alone. Young students need to learn how to "read" both words and graphics.

Reading Graphics helps them do just that. It begins by explaining what graphics are—pictures that give information. The next four pages give students clues that will help them read four specific kinds of graphics: signs, diagrams, tables, and bar graphs.

Rationale

✔ **To be literate, students need to be able to "read" both graphic and verbal information.**

✔ **Understanding graphic information requires different skills than those used in reading alone.**

✔ **Working with graphics gives students new ways to learn and express themselves.**

Major Concepts

✱ Pictures that give information are called graphics; there are many kinds of graphics. (page 171)

✱ Signs, diagrams, tables, and bar graphs share information in separate ways. (pages 172-175)

Planning Notes

Materials: Paper, pencils, a variety of textbooks and trade books that contain simple diagrams, charts, and graphs

Reading/Writing Connections: Books by Gail Gibbons and Richard Scarry are filled with charts and diagrams.

Across-the-Curriculum Possibilities: Students can use their own textbooks and reading materials to learn about graphics. They can create tables to sort information about any subject. They can draw diagrams in language arts (maps and clusters), science (animal habitats), and social studies (mail delivery system). The time line, beginning on page 322 of the handbook, is another graphic that can be discussed.

Reading New Words

(handbook pages 176-179)

*There are books to grow in
and books to know in, . . .*

*Books you're glad you found
and books you can't put down, . . .*

These words from the opening pages of *Write Away* invite us to imagine a young reader experiencing the joy of reading. Children who know what to do with the new words they meet, who read with ease, will become children who love to read.

Reading New Words is a chapter devoted to helping all students read with more ease. They are shown how to look for context clues, how to sound out words, and how to look for word parts they already know. If none of this works, students are encouraged to ask for help.

Rationale

✔ **Young readers need several strategies for reading new words.**

✔ **Beginning readers need to learn how to use sound/symbol correspondences, letter patterns, and context clues to read new words.**

✔ **The information in this chapter spans several developmental reading levels and will benefit most students.**

Major Concepts

❋ There are many ways to read new words. (page 176)

❋ Big words include familiar letter patterns (small words from word families); syllables; and roots, prefixes, and suffixes. (pages 177-179)

Planning Notes

Materials: Reading materials that both match and challenge your students' reading abilities

Reading/Writing Connections: Students will enjoy reading or listening to *Once Upon a Time . . .* , edited by Reading Is Fundamental Foundation (Putnam 1986). In it are stories all about learning to read by Tomie de Paola, Beverly Cleary, and many more authors.

Technology Connections: *Reader Rabbit 1 Deluxe* CD-ROM, *Reader Rabbit 2 Deluxe* CD-ROM, and *Reader Rabbit 3 Deluxe* CD-ROM (The Learning Company) all build reading skills. The Living Books: *Arthur's Birthday* and *Little Monster at School* Bundle CD-ROM (Brøderbund) are two lively stories that also teach reading skills. They are available in Spanish and English.

Chapter Links: "Using Phonics," pages 187-197.
"Making New Words," page 198-201.
"Reading to Understand," pages 180-185

Reading to Understand

(handbook pages 180-185)

In order to learn the skills and strategies for comprehending both fiction and nonfiction, beginning learners need to read materials that are meaningful for them. Reading enjoyment will lead to confidence, and lay the foundation for a steady, lifelong reading habit.

Reading to Understand offers students strategies for becoming more thoughtful readers. The chapter focuses mainly on strategies (called plans) that will help them read, learn, and remember more from nonfiction or fact books. It includes before, during, and after reading activities, both verbal and graphic.

Rationale

✔ Students need to learn how to become independent and thoughtful readers.

✔ Beginning readers need to learn the different strategies for approaching fiction and nonfiction books.

✔ Students who use before, during, and after reading strategies will improve their reading comprehension.

Major Concepts

✱ There are many plans (strategies) to help young students read, learn, and remember. (page 180)

✱ Reading strategies can be modeled/taught/learned in the context of classroom reading instruction. (pages 181-185)

Planning Notes

Materials: A collection of nonfiction books and magazines, chart paper

Chapter Link: "Reading New Words," pages 176-179

Using Phonics

(handbook pages 187-197)

Phonics is a process by which young readers can decode words using sound/symbol relationships. Along with other strategies, phonics needs to be taught in the context of reading, writing, and spelling activities.

Using Phonics contains simple charts and key words for the consonant and vowel sounds in the English language. The chapter covers the basic grapho-phonemic elements that young students will find useful in their language arts studies.

Rationale

✔ **Phonics is one of the strategies used by readers, writers, and spellers.**

✔ **Phonics promotes early word-identification skills.**

✔ **Phonemic awareness (the ability to hear and differentiate between different sounds, syllables, and words) can be taught in a variety of ways.**

Major Concepts

✳ Consonant sounds include initial and final sounds, blends, and digraphs. (pages 188-191)

✳ Vowel sounds include long and short sounds, r-controlled vowels, and diphthongs. (pages 192-197)

Planning Notes

Materials: A collection of books using patterned and rhymed wordage, poetry books, chart paper

Chapter Links: "Reading New Words," pages 176-179
"Making New Words," pages 198-201

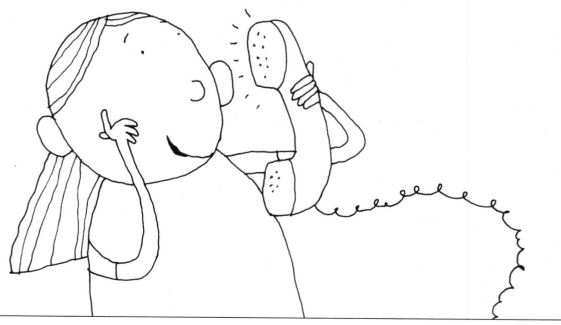

Making New Words

*(handbook
pages 198-201)*

As children learn about the meanings of base words and word parts, they gain independence as readers and writers. Knowing how to combine prefixes, suffixes, and roots helps them to read and write new words.

Making New Words explains exactly what roots, prefixes, and suffixes are. It also gives the meaning of certain prefixes and suffixes and shows how they change the meaning of a base word.

Rationale

✔ **Knowing about prefixes and suffixes helps students figure out the meanings of words.**

✔ **Knowledge of frequently used prefixes and suffixes helps young learners read and write.**

Major Concepts

✳ Prefixes are parts added to the beginning of a word.
(pages 198-199 and 201)

✳ Suffixes are parts added to the end of a word.
(pages 198 and 200-201)

Planning Notes

Chapter Links: "Reading New Words," pages 176-179
"Using Phonics," pages 187-197

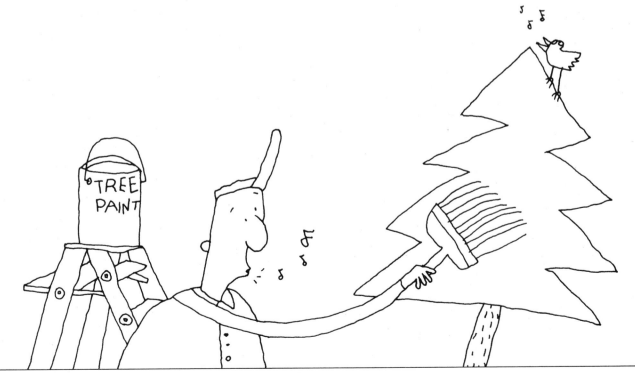

Making Contractions

(handbook pages 202-203)

Children often use contractions in their conversations. When they use them in their writing they need to be able to spell them.

Making Contractions begins by telling students what a contraction is—a shorter word made from one or two longer words. On the facing page there is a list of common contractions.

Rationale

✔ Contractions are commonly used in speaking and writing.

✔ The spellings of contractions follow a pattern.

Major Concepts

✱ A contraction is a shorter word made from one or two longer words. (page 202)

✱ The spellings of contractions always include an apostrophe. (page 203)

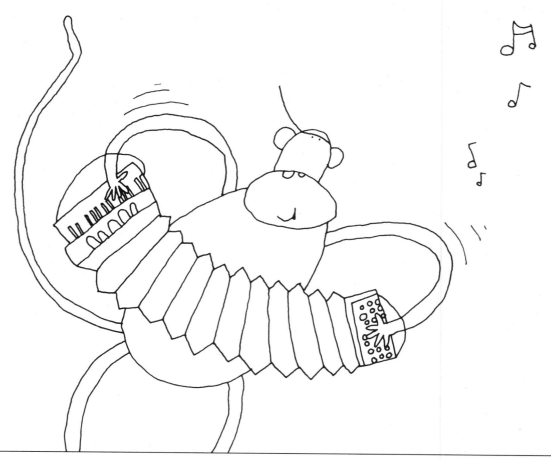

Using a Glossary

*(handbook
pages 204-205)*

Using a glossary is an important stepping-stone to using a dictionary. Young readers are often introduced to glossaries for the first time as they look through their new textbooks.

Using a Glossary will help children learn about the format and purpose of glossaries. A glossary is described as a little dictionary in the back of a book that tells about special words used in the book. Elements of a glossary include guide words, spellings, meanings, and example sentences. A model glossary page is provided.

Rationale

✔ **Knowing how to use a glossary is an important reference skill.**

✔ **Students will use glossaries for word meanings, spellings, and usage in many content areas.**

Major Concepts

✽ A glossary is like a little dictionary in the back of a book. (page 204)

✽ A glossary page includes guide words, correct spelling of entry words, meanings, and sentences using each entry word. (page 204)

Learning to View

*(handbook
pages 207-211)*

Teachers, perhaps more than anyone else, know what a huge role television plays in most children's lives. Given the amount of time children spend watching TV, they need the skills to view it critically.

Learning to View begins by explaining that students can learn from TV—especially from TV specials. The following two pages give students a three-part (before-during-after) plan for watching TV specials. Next, a graphic organizer shows the two main types of programs: real reports and made-up stories. The chapter's last page tells about some of the selling techniques used in commercials.

Rationale

✔ **To learn from TV specials, students need to be active viewers.**

✔ **To learn from TV in general, students need to differentiate between factual and make-believe programming.**

✔ **To be good consumers, students need to be aware of the purpose of commercials and some of the techniques they use.**

Major Concepts

✱ TV is not just for fun—it can help students learn. (page 207)

✱ Students can learn by using a three-part plan when they view TV specials. (pages 208-209)

✱ Most TV programs are real reports or made-up stories. (page 210)

✱ Commercials use different methods to persuade people to buy things. (page 211)

Planning Notes

Materials: A 10- to 15-minute special-interest video or a portion of a videotaped TV special (preferably about a subject students are studying), a video of popular TV commercials (optional)

Across-the-Curriculum Possibilities: Viewing skills help students learn across the curriculum. They will have many opportunities to view TV specials and special-interest videos related to science, social studies, and history.

School and Community Uses: Viewing television, including commercials, can serve as an important topic for a family discussion. Children might take their handbooks home and read the "Learning to View" chapter with a family member.

Learning to Listen

(handbook pages 212-213)

Second graders can appreciate the difference between hearing and listening. For instance, there may be a sound in the classroom that all students can hear (a clock ticking, feet shuffling under desks, etc.), but they ignore it. On the other hand, when they pay attention to the ticking or the shuffling they are listening.

Learning to Listen begins with some lighthearted observation about ears, also stressing their importance in allowing you to listen. And since listening is a great way to learn, these tips are provided for being a good listener: look at the person who is speaking, listen for key words, listen for directions, and ask questions.

Rationale

✔ **Good listening skills promote success in school and in life.**

✔ **Specific strategies can enhance listening skills.**

Major Concepts

✱ **Listening is a great way to learn.** (page 212)

✱ **Looking at the speaker will help students follow along better.** (page 213)

✱ **Listening for key words will help students remember facts.** (page 213)

✱ **Listening for directions will help students know what to do.** (page 213)

✱ **Asking questions will help students understand.** (page 213)

Planning Notes

Materials: Paper, crayons, pencils

Reading/Writing Connections: Read a familiar story aloud, asking your students to listen for particular details. Then, when you're finished, challenge them to write down the facts they remember. (For instance, read *Goldilocks and the Three Bears*, asking them to remember three things Goldilocks did in the house before the bears returned.)

School and Community Uses: Students need good listening skills at assemblies and on field trips. Ask your students to listen for important facts and information during these events. Afterward, they can report back to you.

Technology Connections: Set up a learning center devoted to listening skills. For example, you could have stories and short informational talks available on tape, with questions for students to answer after listening.

Learning to Interview

(handbook pages 214-217)

"The art of interviewing is the art of learning how to learn from other people," writes Donald Graves in *Investigate Nonfiction*. "It is one of the learner's most important tools for growing." It integrates all the major components of language arts (speaking, listening, reading, and writing), *and* it's fun. After all, asking questions is second nature to second graders.

The first page of **Learning to Interview** identifies interviewing as a learning tool. The next three pages discuss the steps in the interview process.

Rationale

✔ **Interviewing is an important way for students to learn.**

✔ **Interviewing sharpens speaking and listening skills.**

Major Concepts

✱ Interviewing is a fun way to learn. (page 214)

✱ Before the interview, write down questions to ask. (page 215)

✱ During the interview, listen and take notes. (page 216)

✱ After the interview, share what you have learned. (page 217)

Planning Notes

Materials: Videotape of an interview (optional), reporter's notebooks for students (optional)

Reading/Writing Connections: Reading interview reports will help students appreciate this learning tool. Here are three possible sources of interviews: *Hip* magazine includes an interview with a student in every issue. *Kid City* sometimes publishes interviews in question-and-answer format. The "Kids Did It" feature in *National Geographic World* is based on interviews with young learners.

Across-the-Curriculum Possibilities: Students can conduct interviews across the curriculum for social studies, math, science, art, and so on. For example, in social studies, students can interview senior citizens to learn about school life in the past.

Performing Stories

*(handbook
pages 218-223)*

Performing stories is an entertaining way to bring a writer's work to life. Students can use their own or others' stories and work cooperatively to create their scripts. Preparing to perform a story hones reading, listening, and speaking skills.

Performing Stories begins by defining reader's theater. Step-by-step directions are then given for planning a performance. Next, part of a model story is shared, along with a script created from the story. Tips for performing are listed, and finally, the second part of the model story is presented. Students are challenged to create a script for it, and then perform the entire piece.

Rationale

✔ **Learning to speak in front of an audience is an important life skill.**

✔ **Performing stories provides a good opportunity for students to cooperate and work toward a common goal.**

✔ **Transforming narrative writing into script form encourages careful reading and thinking.**

Major Concepts

✱ In reader's theater, students don't need to memorize lines . . . they read them. (page 218)

✱ A story with a lot of dialogue can more easily be converted into a reader's theater script. (page 219)

✱ The nonspeaking parts (background, setting, etc.) will be read by a narrator. (page 219)

Planning Notes

Materials: Collection of familiar folktales and fairy tales (possible script material), easel, paper and pencils, poster paper, construction paper

Technology Connections: As your students begin to rehearse for their final performances, you can videotape their practice session. Then review the tape together to discuss both the strengths and the areas in need of improvement. Seeing themselves perform is a helpful way for students to discover elements of stage presence, voice projection, and overall performance.

School and Community Uses: Your students can enjoy the "roar of the crowd." After they have polished their performances, invite parents and other classes to be part of the audience. Decide on several performance times and circulate an invitation sign-up sheet among other teachers. Let parents know about the times of the shows. Set up plenty of chairs, make room on the floor, and have fun performing stories!

Telling Stories

*(handbook
pages 224–227)*

Telling stories is both an enjoyable language experience and a learning opportunity for young children. Besides offering a creative experience for the tellers and the listeners, storytelling develops oral fluency. It also gives children the experience of getting up before a real audience.

The chapter *Telling Stories* introduces children to a model story, "The Three Billy Goats Gruff." Then it gives tips for making this favorite tale or any other story into an opportunity for storytelling.

Rationale

✔ **Telling stories introduces children to the simple joy of listening to and telling a good story.**

✔ **Telling stories helps children express ideas creatively and with fluency.**

✔ **Telling stories enhances children's understanding of the elements of a narrative.**

Major Concepts

✱ **Folktales, fairy tales, and legends make excellent material for storytellers.** (pages 224–226)

✱ **Storytelling tips offer guidance for anyone who wants to tell a story.** (page 227)

Planning Notes

Materials: A variety of folktales and fairy tales, cards or half-sheets of paper, simple materials—sticks, yarn, and fabric scraps—for creating props and puppets

Reading/Writing Connections: Telling stories necessarily involves knowing the setting, the characters, and the plot of a story. Having this experience will benefit the child as a story writer, too.

Across-the-Curriculum Possibilities: As children learn to tell folktales and fairy tales, they can also learn about the history of some of these stories. When possible, discuss the origins of the tales you are reading and telling in your class. For example, the award-winning book *A Story, a Story* by Gail E. Haley (Atheneum 1970) tells about the beginnings of the "spider tales" of Africa.

School and Community Uses: Children can form small storytelling "troupes" and share their stories with other classes, at assemblies, for parent groups, or on special visitor days. This gives them an authentic reason for practicing and following the storytelling tips on page 227—a real audience.

Giving Oral Reports

(handbook pages 228-229)

Children love sharing information about things they are interested in and know a lot about. They may have collections, enjoy hobbies, or belong to a special club. Any of these could serve as the basis for an oral report.

Giving Oral Reports is a short chapter with some very specific guidelines for children. It begins by explaining that an oral report is part telling and part showing. There are also some practical suggestions and steps for both planning and delivering a report.

Rationale

✔ **Oral reports are a natural way for children to express their interests and knowledge.**

✔ **Giving a good oral report requires planning.**

Major Concepts

✷ **An oral report is part telling and part showing.** (page 228)

✷ **Planning an oral report includes choosing a subject and gathering facts.** (page 229)

✷ **A few tips can help students do a good job of giving reports.** (page 229)

Planning Notes

Materials: Note cards or paper, simple props like hats and scarves

Early Literacy Connections: Most young children have had the opportunity to participate in a show-and-tell activity. Usually this is a simple sharing time requiring little preparation. However, these experiences can serve as the foundation for more formal oral reports. With the help of a few planning guidelines, your students will soon be delving into interesting topics, improving their oral language skills, and enriching their vocabularies.

Technology Connections: If it is possible to do so, videotape your students' reports. With your gentle guidance, they will learn a lot about good oral language habits, and thoroughly enjoy seeing themselves on screen.

Getting Organized

(handbook pages 231-235)

Students need organizational skills throughout their lives. Graphic organizers are excellent tools for organizing their thinking and writing.

Getting Organized begins by explaining that students need to organize their thoughts. The chapter then introduces four simple graphic organizers: a cluster, a describing wheel, a Venn diagram, and a story map.

Rationale

✔ **Students need to understand that getting organized is an important step in thinking and writing.**

✔ **Graphic organizers can help students learn, understand, and remember.**

✔ **Graphic organizers can help structure thinking.**

Major Concepts

✱ Getting organized is an important part of thinking. (page 231)

✱ Clustering helps organize details. (page 232)

✱ Describing wheels help organize descriptions. (page 233)

✱ Venn diagrams help make comparisons. (page 234)

✱ Story maps help students remember a story. (page 235)

Planning Notes

Technology Connections: Students can use *Kid Pix* from Brøderbund Software, Inc., and *Inspiration 4.0: The Easiest Way to Brainstorm and Write* from Inspiration Software, Inc. (both available in IBM and Macintosh versions) to create graphic organizers.

Across-the-Curriculum Possibilities: *Graphic Organizers* by Karen Bromley, Linda Irwin-De Vitis, and Marcia Modlo (Scholastic 1995) discusses using graphic organizers in the classroom for science, language arts, social studies, math, and in planning and assessment.

Working in Groups

(handbook pages 236-237)

As children begin to learn about their communities, they see that community life involves people working together. Children can begin learning this important skill.

Working in Groups begins by giving examples of the kinds of people who work in groups. It explains that working in groups helps people finish big jobs. It also reminds students that group members must get along and try hard. Tips for group work are provided, and the chapter concludes with a sample group plan for completing a task together.

Rationale

✔ **Working in groups helps students accomplish more than they could do alone.**

✔ **Knowing how to be a part of a group is an important life skill.**

✔ **Students need to learn how to describe tasks, share ideas, and take turns.**

Major Concepts

✱ Some big jobs can only be finished by working in groups. (page 236)

✱ Everybody in a group must get along and try hard. (page 236)

✱ A group plan helps keep everyone on the right track to finish a job. (page 237)

Planning Notes

Reading/Writing Connections: Students can work in groups as they discuss books they've read. *Invitations: Changing as Teachers and Learners K-12* by Regie Routman (Heinemann 1991) provides organization tips and strategies for grouping children in your classroom.

Early Literacy Connections: If students work on a group project that involves writing, encourage them to depend on each other to produce an error-free product. Provide spelling dictionaries and other word lists for easy reference.

School and Community Uses: The first paragraph in this chapter lists several types of people who work in groups. Challenge your students to create a list of other people in their school and community who work in groups. Discuss how each group uses teamwork to get a job done.

Taking Tests

*(handbook
pages 238-243)*

Although formal test-taking is a new experience for early primary-grade children, some students take tests in stride while others approach them with fear and trembling. Test-taking skills can lessen fears, give students a sense of competency, and help everyone do better on tests.

Taking Tests begins by acknowledging two great truths about tests: They're not necessarily fun, but they are important. The four pages that follow give tips for taking matching, multiple-choice, fill-in-the-blank, and short-answer tests. The chapter's last page lists tips that will help students tackle all kinds of tests.

Rationale

✔ **All students take tests and need test-taking skills.**

✔ **Students with good test-taking skills find tests less intimidating.**

✔ **Students with good test-taking skills achieve scores that are a more accurate reflection of what they know.**

Major Concepts

✱ Tests may not be fun, but they are important. (page 238)

✱ Careful reading and clear thinking are important test-taking skills. (pages 239-242)

✱ Listening to directions and asking questions before beginning a test are two important tips for test takers. (page 243)

Handbook MINILESSONS

Minilessons can transform any classroom into an active learning environment. (We define a minilesson as instruction that lasts about 10-15 minutes and covers a single idea or a core of basic information.) Minilessons can be delivered from the front of the room and include the entire class. They can also be individualized or implemented in writing groups. Ideally, each lesson will address a specific need your students have at a particular time. This makes the lesson meaningful and successful.

In this section, there are minilessons listed for most of the chapters in the handbook. You will find these short exercises invaluable as you plan activities related to the handbook.

The Process of Writing

It's fun to write! . . . . **Starting to Write**

OPEN your handbook to page 13. The kids are smiling about writing. **TELL** a classmate what you like about writing. Then **WRITE** one sentence telling what you like about writing.

Dear Abby, ... **Starting to Write**

READ pages 14 and 15 and **FIND OUT** what Lindy and Roger are saying about writing. On a piece of paper **DRAW** a picture of yourself. Then **DRAW** a speech balloon. In the balloon **WRITE** your own advice about writing.

A Cluster of Ideas . . . . **Using the Writing Process**

On page 22 **READ** how Casey planned her story about Muffy. **CHOOSE** a subject you would like to write about. (It could be your favorite animal!) **MAKE** a cluster like the one in your handbook. **USE** it to list ideas you could put in a story.

I've got an idea! . . . . **Keeping an Idea Notebook**

On page 28 in your handbook, you will find sample pages from two idea notebooks. **THINK** about some things that happened to you this past week. **CHOOSE** two things. **WRITE** them in your idea notebook.

How will your story end? . . . **Keeping an Idea Notebook**

REVIEW the tips on page 29 for using an idea notebook. **PICK** an idea from your idea notebook. **TELL** a partner about your idea. **HAVE** your partner ask you questions about your idea. **WRITE** your partner's questions down. Then **SWITCH** places and **DO** the same thing for your partner.

What's it about? . . . . **Planning Your Writing**

PRETEND your teacher asked you to write an all-about-me story. (There's a chapter in your handbook called "Writing All-About-Me Stories." It begins on page 76.) **THINK** of three subjects you could write about. **WRITE** down your ideas. You may use new ideas or ideas from your idea notebook.

Make a story map. . . . . **Planning Your Writing**

PRETEND you are going to write an all-about-me story. **CHOOSE** a subject to write about. **THINK** of all the parts you will want to include in your story. **MAKE** a story map showing the parts. **SEE** the story map on page 235 in your handbook for help.

We went to the zoo! . . . . **Writing the First Draft**

READ the following sentences about a trip to the zoo. They are in the wrong order. Then **WRITE** them in the correct order, so the story makes sense.

> We saw lions, elephants, and monkeys!
>
> After lunch Dad bought cotton candy.
>
> But I hope I get to go back again.
>
> Yesterday I went to the zoo with my dad.
>
> At the end I was tired.

Let's get started. . . . . **Writing the First Draft**

READ page 33 in your handbook to find out about writing a first draft. **PRETEND** that you are going to write a story about a favorite place. **WRITE** the first sentence of your story, beginning with a fact. Then **WRITE** a different first sentence, beginning with a question.

Is a beach made of dirt? . . . . **Revising Your Writing**

When you revise, you make your writing better. **READ** the paragraph below. **LOOK** for parts you think could be written better. On a piece of paper, **REWRITE** the paragraph. You can **ADD** things, **CHANGE** things, or **TAKE OUT** things. (See page 36 in your handbook for help.)

Today my family went to the beach. Last week my sister got sick at school. I played in the dirt and in the waves I found lots of things. I hope we go back some day, but now I'm going to watch a video.

Two heads are better than one. **Writing Conferences**

OPEN your handbook to page 38. **READ** about writing conferences. Then **CLOSE** your book. In your own words, **TELL** a partner how writing conferences can help you with your writing.

Proofreading Partners. . . . . **Checking for Errors**

TURN to page 41 in your handbook. **CHOOSE** a story or poem from your writing portfolio. **READ** your story or poem to a partner. Make sure you both can see the paper. **CORRECT** any mistakes you and your partner find. **USE** the checklist on page 41 to help you. Then, together, **CHECK** something your partner wrote.

I fixed it! . . . . **Checking for Errors**

First **READ** page 41 in your handbook. Then **READ** the
sentences below. **CIRCLE** the mistakes in each sentence.
Hint: There are two mistakes in each sentence.

1. Billy ran across the gras to catch the ball
2. There are thre kittens in maria's basket.
3. What do you want to play today, billy
4. i can't wait for my dad to get hom.
5. we went to the lake for a weak.

Greeting Cards . . . . **Publishing Your Writing**

CHOOSE a poem from your writing portfolio. **MAKE** a holiday
card or a birthday card. **WRITE** your poem on the card.
DRAW a picture, too. **GIVE** your card to someone you like.
You're a published writer!

Picture-Perfect Bird . . . . **Publishing Your Writing**

OPEN your handbook to page 44. **READ** the poem "Quetzal."
LOOK at the picture with the poem. Now **CHOOSE** one of
your poems and **ADD** a picture.

Name or Tell . . . . **Writing Sentences**

Below are some parts of sentences. **READ** the parts. In the blank **WRITE** the part that is missing. Then **UNDERLINE** the naming part in each sentence.

1. David _____ .

2. _____ went out to play.

3. Two ducks _____ .

4. The boys _____ .

5. My mom _____ .

6. _____ ran to the bus.

I agree. . . . . **Writing Sentences**

The telling parts (verbs) of the sentences below aren't correct. **READ** each sentence. **FIND** the verbs. Then **REWRITE** the sentences with the correct verb.

1. I <u>draws</u> pictures.

2. My family <u>go</u> to the movies.

3. The monkeys <u>swings</u> through the branches.

4. The firefighter <u>climb</u> the ladder.

5. They <u>claps</u> their hands.

And . . . . Writing Longer Sentences

READ the sentences below. **COMBINE** each pair of sentences into one longer sentence. **OPEN** your handbook to page 53 if you need help.

1. Peter lives near the school. Mary lives near the school.

2. Ben went to the store. Ben got new shoes.

What's your favorite game? . . . . . Writing Paragraphs

Below are parts of four sentences. All the sentences make a paragraph. The first sentence is the topic sentence. The next two sentences are the body. The last sentence is the closing.

COMPLETE each sentence by filling in the blank. **OPEN** your handbook to page 55 if you need help.

My favorite game is _____ .

I like it because _____ . The last

time I played _____ . I can't wait to

_____ again!

Strawberry Pizza . . . . Writing Paragraphs

WRITE a paragraph about your favorite food. **NAME** your topic in the first sentence. **TELL** more about it in the middle sentences. Then **WRITE** a closing sentence. (**OPEN** your handbook to page 55 if you need help.)

The Forms of Writing

Three Topics . . . . Writing in Journals

OPEN your handbook to pages 66 and 67. **READ** what Josh wrote in his journal. On a piece of paper **WRITE** three topics you would like to write about in your journal. Try to **THINK** of things Josh didn't think of.

Dear Me, ... Writing in Journals

WRITE a journal entry for today. You may **WRITE** about something you did or about someone you talked to. You may **WRITE** about a feeling you have right now. **LOOK** at pages 66 and 67 in your handbook if you need help.

Yesterday, Today, Tomorrow . . . . Writing in Journals

In a journal, you can write about what happened in the past, or about what is happening right now. You can also dream about the future. **WRITE** a journal entry for each of these times "yesterday," "today," and "tomorrow."

Ha! Ha! . . . . **Writing Friendly Notes**

Do you want to make someone laugh? **WRITE** a note to that person. Tell a joke or a funny story in the note. **ADD** a picture. See if your note makes the person laugh. **FIND OUT** about friendly notes on pages 68-71 in your handbook.

Thanks, Teacher! . . . . **Writing Friendly Notes**

WRITE a thank-you note to your teacher. **TELL** your teacher about a lesson that you liked. Say thank you for helping you learn. **FIND OUT** about friendly notes on pages 68-71 in your handbook.

Drop me a line. . . . . **Writing Friendly Letters**

CHOOSE two people you would like to write to. **WRITE** their names on a sheet of paper. Then **PICK** one of the names. **LIST** two or three things you would like to tell that person in a friendly letter.

Dear Uncle Jake, ... **Writing Friendly Letters**

CHOOSE someone who would like to get a friendly letter from you. **THINK** of some good news to tell that person. Then **WRITE** it in a letter. **CHECK** pages 72-75 in your handbook for ideas about writing a friendly letter.

A Good Start .... Writing All-About-Me Stories

THINK of an idea for an all-about-me story. **WRITE** a first sentence for your story. **MAKE** the sentence exciting and interesting. (There's a good example at the top of page 79 in your handbook.) **TRADE** sentences with a partner. **READ** each other's sentences. Can you help each other make the sentences better?

Review the review. .... Writing About Books

READ the book review on page 83 in your handbook. **COPY** one sentence that tells what the book is about. Then **COPY** one sentence that tells what the writer likes about the book.

What's so great about it? ..... Writing About Books

THINK of your favorite book. **WRITE** one sentence that tells what the book is about. Then **WRITE** one sentence that tells something you like about the book.

A Number of Rhymes .... Making Counting Books

OPEN your handbook to page 91. **READ** about writing with numbers and rhymes. Stan made rhymes for the numbers *one, two,* and *three.* Now **LIST** words that rhyme with *four* and *five.* **THINK** of as many rhyming words as you can.

Pete goes to Disney World! . . . . **Writing News Stories**

You can get ideas for a news story by asking five questions. **INTERVIEW** a partner. **WRITE** your partner's answers to the questions below.

1. Who are you?
2. What is the name of your favorite place?
3. Where is this place?
4. When did you go to this place?
5. What did you do there?

Now **WRITE** the first sentence of a news story. Remember to give the most important information in this sentence.

Why is your truck yellow? . . . **Writing Business Letters**

WRITE a business letter to your local fire station. **ASK** the firefighters to send you information about fire safety. Also **ASK** them any questions you have. **FOLLOW** the form of a business letter on pages 98 and 99 in your handbook. Ask a grown-up to help you get your letter ready to mail.

How do you do that? . . . . **Writing Directions**

What do you know how to do? Can you send a fax or draw a picture of a person? **CHOOSE** something you know how to do. On a piece of paper, **WRITE** directions telling how to do it. **FIND OUT** about writing directions on pages 102-105 in your handbook.

Turn left at the chalkboard. . . . . . . **Writing Directions**

WRITE directions from your desk to another place in your classroom (the door, a pet cage, the reading center, and so on). **GIVE** your directions to a classmate. **SEE** if that person can find the place you picked. **FIND OUT** about writing directions on pages 102-105 in your handbook.

Sign up for the field trip. . . . . **Making Posters**

CHOOSE an event and make a poster about it. It could be a birthday party, a field trip, or something happening in your class. On a piece of paper, **PLAN** your poster. Then **DRAW** a copy of your plan on a large piece of paper or poster board. **PUT** the poster up somewhere for everyone to see.

Please don't litter. . . . . **Making Posters**

CHOOSE something to share in a poster. (**LOOK** at page 108 in your handbook. The person who made that poster wants people to protect the rain forest.) **WRITE** what you want to share on your poster. Then **DRAW** a picture to go with your writing. Make sure the picture helps the reader understand your idea.

Real or Make-Believe . . . . **Using the Library**

DO this minilesson with a partner. The words below tell about books. **READ** each set of words. **WRITE** an **F** in the blank if the book is fiction. **WRITE** an **N** if it is nonfiction. **WRITE** a **B** if it is a biography. **WRITE** an **R** if it is a reference book. **USE** pages 112 and 113 in your handbook to help you.

1. The life story of Thomas Edison _____

2. A book of maps of different countries _____

3. A story about a little girl who finds a dinosaur in her yard _____

4. A book about different kinds of bears _____

5. The life story of George Washington _____

What do you want to know? .... **Writing Reports**

READ page 121 in your handbook to learn about gathering grids. **THINK** of something you would like to know more about. **MAKE** a gathering grid for your topic. **USE** a big piece of paper. **WRITE** the name of your topic in the upper left corner. Then **WRITE** four or five questions about your topic. **LEAVE** enough room for your answers.

Teeter-Totter, Monkey Bars, Swings ..... **Making Picture Dictionaries**

TURN to page 126 to find out how to make picture dictionaries. Then **BEGIN** your own picture dictionary about a playground. **WRITE** down one thing you find on a playground. **WRITE** a sentence about it. Then **DRAW** a picture of the thing. There you have it—the first page of your picture dictionary.

My Favorite Words .... **Making Picture Dictionaries**

CHOOSE a subject for a picture dictionary. **OPEN** your handbook to page 129 if you need help. Think of words you could put in your picture dictionary. **LIST** as many words as you can. **PUT** a star by the words you like best.

Begin and End at Home . . . . **Writing Circle Stories**

TELL someone a story about yourself. Begin at your house, leave your house to do something special, and then come back to your house. After you **TELL** the story, **DRAW** pictures of each part. Later, **WRITE** your circle story.

Where's the caterpillar? . . . . . **Writing Add-On Stories**

TELL an add-on story. **BEGIN** with this sentence: "The caterpillar is gone!" **ASK** three of your classmates to **GUESS** what happened to the caterpillar. Then end the story by **TELLING** how the caterpillar became a butterfly. You and your classmates have just told a type of add-on story!

Lessons from Animals . . . . **Writing Fables**

A fable teaches a lesson. **THINK** of the lessons that different animals could teach you. What about a lesson from a cat, a dog, a squirrel, a goldfish, or a goat? **CHOOSE** two animals. Then **WRITE** a lesson that these animals could teach you.

I lost my . . . . **Writing Mysteries**

THINK about a time you lost something. Then try to **REMEMBER** how you found what you lost. **WRITE** down what happened. If you **MAKE UP** some new parts and add some new characters, you'll be writing a mystery.

The Tools of Learning

Time for a Conference . . . . **Reading Graphics**

A sign sometimes uses pictures *and* words. **MAKE** a sign that tells your teacher you want to have a writing conference. You can **USE** any words and pictures you would like.

Compound Words . . . . **Reading New Words**

READ the words below. The words in row one are the first half of a compound word. The words in row two are the second part of a word. **MAKE** as many compound words as you can, combining words in row one with words in row two.

1. book   butter   cow   honey   dog   ground

2. hog   mark   house   milk   comb   boy

Retell it. . . . . **Reading to Understand**

READ "My Interview" on page 217 in your handbook. Then **WRITE** about what you read. This is called a retelling. Here are two questions to help you write your retelling: What is the most important thing you learned? What other things did you learn?

Know, Want to Know . . . . **Reading to Understand**

PRETEND you will be reading a book about turtles. **MAKE** a chart like the one below. Under "Know," **LIST** three things you already know about turtles. Under "Want to Know," **LIST** two things you want to know about turtles. (At another time, try a KWL chart. **SEE** page 182 in your handbook.)

Know	Want to Know

Consonant Twisters . . . . **Using Phonics**

MAKE a list of words that begin with the "s" sound. **WRITE** a long sentence using as many "s" words as you can. Try to **READ** your tongue twister sentence fast! **DO** this with two other consonant sounds, too.

Add an "e." . . . . **Using Phonics**

You can **CHANGE** short-vowel words to long-vowel words. **ADD** an "e" to each of the words below, and you will have long-vowel words. **WRITE** the long-vowel words on your own paper. Then **WRITE** a funny sentence using two or more of the words.

mad   hat   can   hop   tim   rip   cap   tap

Bragging . . . . **Making New Words**

READ these words. **NOTICE** that each word has the suffix "er" or "est."

bigger   faster   coldest   shorter

taller   thicker   longest   happier

CHOOSE a word and **MAKE UP** a sentence that "brags." For example, you could write "My dog has the longest tail." **WRITE** three bragging sentences and then **SHARE** them with a friend.

Find the match. . . . . **Making Contractions**

READ the sentences below. On a piece of paper **MAKE** a list of the contractions from the sentences. Next to each contraction **WRITE** the two words that the contraction came from. (Pages 202-203 in your handbook can help you.)

1. Don't go near the hole!

2. I can't find my sock.

3. Joe doesn't like chocolate.

4. It's time to go.

5. I've got a new book.

Four Directions . . . . **Learning to Listen**

FIND a partner for a listening game. **GIVE** your partner a piece of paper. **TELL** your partner four things to do. (**SPEAK** slowly!)

1. Fold the paper in half.
2. Fold the paper in half again.
3. Open the paper.
4. Trace the lines with a red crayon.

After this, **ASK** your partner to give you four directions to follow.

Once there was . . . . **Telling Stories**

TELL a story about a nursery rhyme. **TRY** "Jack and Jill" to begin with. Instead of saying the rhyme, **BEGIN** this way: "One day Jack and Jill were going to get some water." Then **TELL** why they were going for water. Then **DESCRIBE** the hill. **EXPLAIN** why Jack and Jill fell. **END** the story by telling how they were rescued.

A Character I Know . . . . **Getting Organized**

READ about a describing wheel on page 233 of your handbook. **DRAW** a describing wheel of your own. **WRITE** the name of a story character in the middle of the wheel. (You could write Goldilocks, Red Riding Hood, or Peter Rabbit.) **WRITE** words that describe your character on the spokes. **DRAW** a picture of your character if you'd like.

Team Up . . . . **Working in Groups**

Together with three classmates, **PLAN** to decorate a bulletin board. (Your teacher will tell you who to work with.) **GET** the group together and **READ** the "Planning Tips" on page 237 in your handbook. **FOLLOW** these tips and **WRITE** a "Group Plan." (Perhaps you will also have a chance to complete the bulletin board.)

The Proofreader's Guide

Worms are wiggly. . . . . **Using Punctuation**

WRITE three telling sentences about worms. **USE** the correct end punctuation.

Dr. for Doctor . . . . **Using Punctuation**

Mr., Mrs., Ms., and Dr. are abbreviations. They are used before people's names.

Example: Mrs. Brown

WRITE your teacher's name with the correct abbreviation before it. Then **WRITE** the names of two other grown-ups you know.

Think of a number. . . . . **Using Punctuation**

ASK a partner to pick an amount of money that is between one dollar and ten dollars. It should have both dollars and cents. **WRITE** the amount in numerals. **USE** a dollar sign, and put a period between dollars and cents.

Example: If your partner says, "Two dollars and ten cents," you write $2.10.

How do you end a question? ..... Using Punctuation

COMPLETE each question below. Make sure to use the correct end punctuation. The first one has been done for you.

1. **Who** <u>spilled paint on the floor?</u>

2. **What** _____

3. **When** _____

4. **Where** _____

5. **Why** _____

6. **How** _____

I got lost at the mall! .... Using Punctuation

An exclamation point is used after a sentence that shows strong feelings. **WRITE** two or three sentences about a time when you were excited, or happy, or scared. **USE** an exclamation point after at least one of your sentences.

Rain, Snow, Wind, and Hail .... Using Punctuation

USE commas correctly as you follow these directions. **WRITE** a sentence that lists four funny things. **WRITE** a sentence that lists four things you learn about in school. **WRITE** a sentence that lists three holidays. **LOOK** at page 251 in your handbook if you need help.

I flew to Cleveland, Ohio. . . . . Using Punctuation

MAKE a list of five cities and states. Make sure to **USE** commas correctly. (**LOOK** at page 250 in your handbook for help.) **SEE** page 306 in your handbook if you want to write five state capitals.

Example: Tallahassee, Florida

Dear Mary, ... Using Punctuation

WRITE a letter to a friend, telling all about your favorite animal. **PUT** commas after the greeting and the closing of your letter. If you need help, **LOOK** at page 250 in your handbook.

Lunchtime! . . . . Using Punctuation

IMAGINE two ants talking about the good snacks they are eating from your picnic basket. **WRITE** the ants' words using quotation marks and other punctuation correctly. **SEE** pages 251 and 253 in your handbook for help.

Two Thumbs Up! . . . . Using Punctuation

ASK a partner two questions: (1) What is your favorite magazine? (2) What is your favorite book? Now **WRITE** two sentences: (1) Tell what your partner's favorite magazine is. (2) Tell what your partner's favorite book is. Be sure to capitalize and punctuate the titles correctly. **SEE** pages 253 and 256 in your handbook for help.

Happy Birthday! . . . . Using Punctuation

ASK three people to tell you what day they were born. **ASK** the year, too. **WRITE** down all the birthdays. Make sure to **USE** commas correctly. **SEE** page 250 in your handbook.

Whose is it? . . . . Using Punctuation

WRITE words with apostrophes to show ownership for the list of nouns below. **SEE** page 252 in your handbook.

Example: the ____dog's____ bone

1. _____ flowers

2. the _____ wagon

3. the _____ socks

4. _____ car

5. _____ desk

6. your _____ picture

7. _____ books

8. my _____ bike

I like holidays. . . . . Checking Mechanics

WRITE sentences about two or three of your favorite holidays. **TELL** what you like best about each holiday. Be sure to **USE** capitals letters correctly. **SEE** page 256 in your handbook.

Example: I love the heart cookies Grandma bakes for Valentine's Day.

Today's the day. . . . . Checking Mechanics

WRITE three sentences. Each sentence should be about a different day of the week. Remember to **USE** capital letters for the days of the week.

Example: Every Saturday we go out for pizza.

Dear Mr. President, ... Checking Mechanics

PRETEND you're writing a letter to the president of the United States. Here is his address: 1600 Pennsylvania Avenue, Washington, DC 20500. **WRITE** the address as if you were putting it on an envelope. **LOOK** at page 258 in your handbook for help.

How many legs does your aunt have? . . . . **Using the Right Word**

TURN to pages 268 and 269 of your handbook. **PICK** one set of words. **READ** the example sentences. On a piece of paper, **COPY** the sentences, but switch the words.

Example: An aunt crawled onto my finger.

My ant likes to tell jokes.

(These sentences are silly, aren't they?)

ASK a friend to read and correct your silly sentences.

Hear, Here . . . . **Using the Right Word**

WORK with a partner. **OPEN** your handbook to pages 270 and 271. **PICK** a set of words, but don't let your partner see. **READ** the first word and sentence out loud to your partner.

Example: "Hear – I like to hear birds sing."

ASK your partner to write down the word. Then check it. Take turns.

S or V . . . . Checking Your Sentences

TURN to page 274 in your handbook. **COMPLETE** the following simple sentences. **ADD** a subject or a verb, whichever is needed.

1. _____ swim.   4. Cars _____ .

2. _____ hurry.   5. Parrots _____ .

3. Children _____ .   6. _____ shines.

Season Sentences . . . . Checking Your Sentences

TURN to page 285 in your handbook. **LOOK** at the list of season/weather words. **PICK** two of the words, and **WRITE** one sentence using both of them.

Example: It is cold in the winter.

The 5 W's . . . . Checking Your Sentences

WRITE five simple questions a partner could answer. **BEGIN** each question with one of the 5 W's. Who . . . ? What . . . ? When . . . ? Where . . . ? Why . . . ?

Example: Who was the first president?

How many nouns? . . . . . . **Understanding Our Language**

OPEN your handbook to page 277 and **READ** about nouns. Next, **READ** the paragraph about the bus on page 127. On a piece of paper, **WRITE** down all the nouns you find in the paragraph. (There are seven nouns in all. Some are singular, and some are plural.)

Not Just Any Old Park . . **Understanding Our Language**

OPEN your handbook to page 60. **READ** the story about visiting the park. On the lines below, **WRITE** each proper noun you find in the story. **SEE** page 277 in your handbook for help.

_____

_____

Is that mine? . . . . **Understanding Our Language**

CHOOSE three things in your classroom that belong to three different people. On a piece of paper, **WRITE** three sentences for the three things. Each should begin with "That is."

Example: That is my teacher's desk.

SEE page 277 in your handbook for help.

It's an elephant. .... Understanding Our Language

Do this minilesson with a partner. **OPEN** your handbook to page 223. **READ** the second part of the story about a yellow elephant. On a piece of paper, **WRITE** down the six different pronouns you see in the story.

Play, Play, Play .... Understanding Our Language

CHOOSE three things you really like to do. **WRITE** a sentence about each thing. **UNDERLINE** the verb in each sentence. **SEE** page 279 in your handbook for help.

Example: I <u>chase</u> my dog down the street.

The History of You ..... Understanding Our Language

THINK of three things you did yesterday. On a piece of paper, **WRITE** three sentences telling what you did. **USE** past tense verbs. **UNDERLINE** the verb in each sentence. **SEE** page 279 in your handbook for help.

Example: I <u>played</u> soccer.

Planning Ahead . . . . **Understanding Our Language**

PRETEND that you can do anything you want to do tomorrow. **WRITE** three sentences telling what you will do. **USE** future tense verbs. **UNDERLINE** the verb in each sentence. **SEE** page 279 in your handbook for help.

Example: I will ride roller coasters all morning.

How does it feel? . . . . **Understanding Our Language**

Some adjectives describe how something feels. **SEE** how many different "feeling" adjectives you can **WRITE** to **DESCRIBE** these words.

WIND   SWEATER   SIDEWALK

_____   _____   _____

_____   _____   _____

_____   _____   _____

Smarter Than the Average Bear . . . . **Understanding Our Language**

Are you smaller than an elephant? Are you bigger than an ant? **WRITE** two sentences that compare you with something else. **USE** adjectives that compare things. **SEE** page 282 in your handbook for help with adjectives that compare.

Examples: bigger, taller, smaller, smarter

January is cold and snowy. . . . . Using Theme Words

OPEN your handbook to page 284. **LOOK** over the words for days and months. **CHOOSE** a day and **WRITE** a sentence about it. Then choose a month and write a sentence about it.

Food Sort . . . . Using Theme Words

TURN to page 286 in your handbook. **READ** the food words. Then make three columns on a piece of paper. Name the columns: Yummy, So-So, and Yuck. **WRITE** each food word in the column of your choice. **COMPARE** your lists with others in your class.

Yummy	So-So	Yuck

It was a dark and sunny night. . . . . Using Theme Words

LOOK over the season/weather words on page 285 in your handbook. On a piece of paper, **WRITE** some nonsense sentences using some of these words. ("Nonsense" means something that doesn't make sense!)

Example: Winter finally came! It was hot and sunny. There were clouds on the ground.

The Student Almanac

The Secret Sign . . . . **Useful Tables and Lists**

Work with a partner. **TURN** to page 291 in your handbook. **LOOK** over the table about sign language. **MAKE UP** a secret message that only you and your partner know. **LEARN** to "say" the message in sign language.

A Different Language . . . . **Useful Tables and Lists**

TURN to page 294 in your handbook. **LOOK** over the table about the Braille alphabet and Braille numbers. **WRITE** your name in Braille. Then **WRITE** a short message. Trade papers with a partner. **DECODE** the words one letter at a time. Then **READ** each other's message.

Shalom, mi amigo. . . . . **Useful Tables and Lists**

Do this minilesson with a partner. **OPEN** your handbook to page 293. **LOOK** over the table. **PRETEND** you are traveling around the world. **TRY** saying hello and good-bye in two of the languages. **ASK** your teacher to help you say the words the first time.

When in Rome . . . . Useful Tables and Lists

OPEN your handbook to page 292. **STUDY** the table of Roman numerals to help you fill in the blanks below.

1. I am _____ years old.

2. A cat has _____ paws.

3. There are _____ planets in our solar system. (*Hint:* The answer is on page 298 in your handbook.)

4. There are _____ states in the United States.

5. There are _____ pennies in a dime.

6. There are _____ pennies in a dollar.

7. A clock shows _____ hours.

8. The first Roman numeral in 1997 would be _____ .

9. A hand has _____ fingers.

10. There are _____ feet in a yard.

A Whale of a Story .... Useful Tables and Lists

OPEN your handbook to page 294. **LOOK** over the table of animal facts. **FIND** the names for the young animals listed below.

1. deer _____

2. goose _____

3. swine _____

4. donkey _____

5. monkey _____

6. whale _____

7. rabbit _____

8. bear _____

9. goat _____

10. sheep _____

The Great Animal Race ...... **Useful Tables and Lists**

OPEN your handbook to page 295. **STUDY** the table. **PRETEND** that all the animals are in a race. **USE** the table to answer the following questions.

1. The two slowest animals will be the

   _____ and the _____ .

2. The two fastest animals will be the

   _____ and the _____ .

3. Which three animals are likely to end in a tie?

   _____

4. If a human joins the race, which four animals will be slower than the human?

   _____   _____

   _____   _____

Planets in Their Places . . . . **Useful Tables and Lists**

OPEN your handbook to page 298. **READ** about the solar system. Also **CHECK OUT** the map on page 299. Then **WRITE** in the missing words.

1. _____ is the largest planet.

2. _____ and Venus are closer to the sun than Earth is.

3. _____ and _____ have rings around them.

4. _____ is the coldest planet.

5. _____ is the farthest from the sun.

6. _____ is more than 10 times bigger than Earth.

7. The smallest planet is _____ .

8. The closest planet to Earth is _____ .

9. All the planets orbit around the _____ .

10. _____ is the slowest-spinning planet.

The Isle of Kid . . . . All About Maps

DRAW a map of a make-believe island. **DECIDE** if you want mountains or lakes on your island. **PUT** a town on the island if you want to. **NAME** your island. **PUT** some symbols on it if you like. **LOOK** at page 301 in your handbook if you need help.

Howdy, neighbor! . . . . All About Maps

OPEN your handbook to page 303. **USE** the map of the continents to help you do this minilesson. **MAKE** a list of the seven continents. **CIRCLE** the two continents that do not touch any other continent. **UNDERLINE** your continent.

Border Lands . . . . All About Maps

TURN to page 305 in your handbook. **FIND** the state you live in on the map. **WRITE** the names of all the other states that touch your state. Now **FIND** Kansas on the map. **WRITE** the names of all the states that touch Kansas.

Capital Cities . . . . All About Maps

Page 306 of your handbook lists all the states and their capitals. First **WRITE** down your own state capital. Name both the city and the state. Then **WRITE** down five more capitals and states in the same way.

Example: Madison, Wisconsin

Bookmarks .... Improving Handwriting

CUT strips of colored paper for making bookmarks. On each bookmark **WRITE** your first and last name as nicely as you can. **DECORATE** your bookmarks. **USE** them to keep your places in your library books and school books.

Pretty Poetry .... Improving Handwriting

FIND a favorite poem that you would like to save. **USE** your best handwriting to copy the poem. **PUT** it somewhere so you can see it. Then **READ** it over and over until you know it by heart.

Crosswords .... Improving Handwriting

MAKE a list of names. It could be friends, family members, pets, or so on. **WRITE** the names across and down in crossword form. (See the examples below.) **MAKE** a poster of your crossword, using your best handwriting.

Example:

```
              R
      L       O              D A V E
      A       G              A
      P A U L I N E          J A N E L L E
      R       R O N          N
      A                      Y V O N N E
```

My Summer with Andre .... **History in the Making**

Andre and his family went on vacation last summer. He traveled all over the United States. Sometimes he forgets the names of the places he visited. Use page 307 of your handbook to **FILL IN** the blanks and help Andre.

1. He went to the largest city.

   What is it called? _____

2. He also visited the largest desert.

   What is the name of that desert? _____

3. He went on a boat ride on the largest lake.

   It is called _____

4. He crossed the longest river on a long bridge.

   That river is called the _____

5. He also went to the largest state.

   What is its name? _____

Extra! Read all about it! . . . . . . **History in the Making**

OPEN your handbook to the time line on page 323.

CHOOSE one event from the 1600's that you think is exciting and important, and **WRITE** it down. Then write down an event from the 1700's, 1800's, and 1900's. Remember to include the years in which the events happened.

Famous Names . . . . **History in the Making**

Below are the names of three famous people. **FIND** each person on the time line in your handbook. (The time line begins on page 323.) **USE** what you learn to write a sentence about each person.

Benjamin Franklin   **Dr. Seuss**   **Jackie Robinson**

First Things First . . . . **History in the Making**

READ about all the events listed during the 1700's. **WRITE** down the three things that interest you the most. Be ready to share your favorite with the class.

Handbook MINILESSONS
Answer Key

This section provides an answer key for the few minilessons requiring specific answers. In most cases, the students' answers for the minilessons will vary.

The Process of Writing

We went to the zoo! (page 87)

Yesterday I went to the zoo with my dad. We saw lions, elephants, and monkeys! After lunch Dad bought cotton candy. At the end I was tired. But I hope I get to go back again.

Is a beach made of dirt? (page 88) (Answers will vary.)

Today my family went to the beach. I played in the sand and in the ocean waves. I built a sand castle with my sister. We found lots of smooth stones and shells. I hope we go back some day.

I fixed it! (page 89)

1. Billy ran across the (gras) to catch the ball(.)
2. There are (thre) kittens in (maria's) basket.
3. What do you want to play today, (billy) (?)
4. (i) can't wait for my dad to get (hom.)
5. (we) went to the lake for a (weak.)

I agree. (page 90)

1. draw   3. swing   5. clap
2. goes   4. climbs

And (page 91)

Peter and Mary live near the school.
Ben went to the store and got new shoes.

The Forms of Writing

Real or Make-Believe (page 97)

1. B   3. F   5. B
2. R   4. N

The Tools of Writing

Compound Words (page 100)

bookmark   buttermilk   cowboy   honeycomb   doghouse   groundhog

Add an "e." (page 102)

made   hate   cane   hope   time   ripe   cape   tape

Find the match. (page 103)

1. Don't   Do not   3. doesn't does not   5. I've   I have
2. can't   can not   4. It's   It is

The Proofreader's Guide

Dear Mr. President, (page 109)

MR PRESIDENT
1600 PENNSYLVANIA AVENUE
WASHINGTON DC 20500

How many nouns? (page 112)

bus, wheels, People, buses, city, buses, people

Not Just Any Old Park (page 112)

Blue Hills Park   Treasure Cave

It's an elephant. (page 113)

I, his, him, he, it, they

The Student Almanac

When in Rome (page 117)

2. IV	4. L	6. C	8. M	10. III
3. IX	5. X	7. XII	9. V	

A Whale of a Story (page 118)

1. fawn	3. piglet	5. boy/girl	7. bunny	9. kid
2. gosling	4. foal	6. calf	8. cub	10. lamb

The Great Animal Race (page 119)

1. snail   giant tortoise
2. osprey   cheetah
3. white-tailed deer, grizzly bear, cat
4. elephant   snake   giant tortoise   snail

Planets in Their Places (page 120)

1. Jupiter
2. Mercury
3. Saturn   Uranus
4. Neptune
5. Pluto
6. Jupiter
7. Pluto
8. Mars
9. sun
10. Venus

My Summer with Andre (page 123)

1. New York City
2. Mojave Desert
3. Lake Superior
4. Mississippi River
5. Alaska

Evaluating/Assessing
MONITORING

The information in this section will help you evaluate your students' work. Included are general assessment guidelines, specific strategies for evaluating writing, and copymasters of tips and guidelines that students can use as they respond to their own and others' writing.

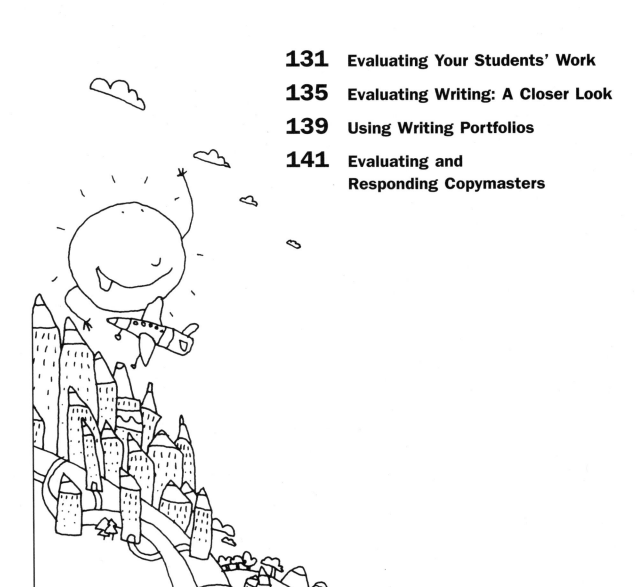

Evaluating Your Students' Work

The ultimate goal of evaluation should be to help students improve their overall language proficiency. The guidelines and strategies that follow have been designed with these important points in mind.

Special Note: To help students become active participants in the evaluation process, make sure that they know how to use *Write Away*. It's especially important that they become familiar with "The Writing Process" section.

How should I evaluate my students?

The best methods of evaluation are those that address the process of learning as much as (or more) than the end products of learning. Evaluation should be . . .

— based on overall performance,
— interesting and functional in design,
— open-ended and flexible in scope, and
— meaningful and relevant to the particular learner.

In other words, the evaluation of students' work should be as *authentic* as possible.

What is meant by authentic assessment?

Authentic assessment is based on the principle that evaluation guides instruction. Authentic assessment is carried out through observations, interactions, and analysis.

— When you *observe* a student at work, notice his or her enthusiasm, diligence, care, creativity, neatness, and so on.
— When you *interact* with a student, informally question him or her about the work in progress. Also engage in small-group discussions and conduct student/teacher conferences.
— When you *analyze* a student's work, carefully examine his or her finished product. Highlight particular strengths; make suggestions for upcoming assignments; note your overall impressions; and award a point total, mark, or comment.

Should I use all three evaluation methods on each activity?

No, it would be next to impossible to observe and interact with students as well as analyze their work for each and every activity. However, we do encourage you to make use of all three methods of assessment throughout the course of the school year.

How should I evaluate writing?

As you know, a great deal has been written about the teaching of writing, including how to evaluate writing as a process rather than an end product. We have encapsulated much of this information, starting on page 135 of this section. Insights into assessing writing in progress (formative evaluation) as well as insights into assessing the end result of writing (summative evaluation) are addressed on these pages.

Recently, much attention has been given to special writing portfolios in which students showcase their best writing for evaluation at the end of a grading period. Portfolios place a significant part of the assessment process in the hands of the student writers because they can select and choose what they want evaluated. Students appreciate the sense of ownership this gives them. Teachers appreciate portfolios because the evaluation process can be used to assess a representative sample of students' products, as opposed to grading every written selection. (Guidelines for using writing portfolios are included in this section, starting on page 139.)

Note: Remember that the type of writing done by the students determines the level of evaluation that is appropriate. Certain forms of personal or exploratory writing should be awarded a basic performance score plus several positive comments. A more complex writing project naturally demands more thorough analysis.

How should I address basic skills?

It has been demonstrated in study after study that learning the basic skills of grammar and punctuation out of context has little relevance for young learners and little carryover to their authentic language experiences. Students learn about their language as they use it in their daily lives, and as they read, write, speak, listen, and think.

When you notice that a student has difficulty with a particular skill, help him or her learn from this problem. There's little incentive to learn if a student is penalized for making particular errors in an individual piece of writing. There's all the incentive in the world to learn if a student is rewarded for attempting to correct the error. Always remember that evaluation guides instruction.

Helping Each Student: If a student writer doesn't remember to use end punctuation marks, you can do a number of things:

— First note the error, showing the student why it is incorrect.

— Then refer the student to the handbook to learn how to correct the error.

— Model for the student "how to" correct the error.

— Also have the student record the error in a special section of a notebook, so he or she will know what to look for in the next piece of writing.

Helping a Small Group: If you feel the error is common to many students in the class, consider assigning a related minilesson. (See pages 85-124 in this guide for minilessons.)

Let students know that you expect them to look for the problem in future writing assignments. Then, when you evaluate their work at the end of the term, check to see what progress they are making.

What about handwriting?

Always remember that handwriting (manuscript and cursive) is not an end in itself. Students use handwriting to express themselves on paper. The main focus of evaluation should be to encourage and help students print and/or write more legibly and fluently over the long term. Students can evaluate their handwriting in final drafts using the handwriting checklist on page 321 in the *Write Away* handbook.

Should I do all of the evaluating?

No, evaluation should be part of the learning process and should involve students as much as possible. Students automatically become involved in the process if they complete self-evaluation sheets or briefly reflect on their learning progress in a notebook or journal. Questions students might ask of themselves include the following: *Did things go as I planned in this activity? What did I like the best about my writing? What caused me the most problems? What could I do to improve my writing the next time we do this type of activity?*

Students can also participate in peer-evaluation conferences or peer-response groups. These conferences work best if students have a predetermined checklist or guide with which to judge their peers' work. (See pages 141-142 in this section for sample conferencing sheets.)

Special Note: Don't expect beginning writers to be careful, insightful, and fair evaluators right from the start. This skill will come only with practice, guided by the teacher. (The *Write Away* student handbook contains information on conferencing with partners.)

Parents should also be involved in the evaluation process. For example, they can be encouraged to react (via written messages or in conferences) to their child's work, whether it be a series of daily assignments or a more important writing selection. Parents can also react to their child's portfolio at the end of a grading period.

Should I assign a grade or mark for each activity?

We certainly don't recommend it. Teachers don't always have the time to review each activity carefully enough to assign a grade. Additionally, grading each activity is not a productive method of evaluating. Grades can hinder learning because they represent a stopping point, an end result. A more open-ended system of evaluation is much more in line with current research of best writing practices.

We believe that a basic "performance" score is sufficient for most of the writing activities. Teachers can assign students a predetermined number of points (5), a comment (Excellent), or a mark (+) upon completion of their work. (The score students receive depends on their basic performance.) We also believe teachers should make at least one specific, positive comment on individual activity sheets.

How should I grade work at the end of the quarter or semester?

If your students keep folders of their work and evaluations, you have a complete collection or sampling for each student. You may also have students showcase their best work in a portfolio. If you noted observations and interactions during various activities, you have your own personal comments and reactions to consider. With the materials you have collected, there will be enough information to assess each student's performance.

Quarter or semester grading ought to reflect a measurement of each student's progress as a language learner—as much as, or even more than, the quality of the end products.

Evaluating Writing: A Closer Look

Several kinds of evaluation interest teachers today. **Formative evaluation** (evaluating while the students are developing their writing) and **summative evaluation** (evaluating the outcome of the students' efforts) are two of these evaluation types. Formative evaluation does not result in a grade; summative evaluation usually does. Some teachers choose to give students a set number of points (a performance score) during different stages in the formative writing process.

Formative Evaluation

Formative evaluation is most often used for writing-to-learn activities, prewriting activities, writing in progress, journal entries, and so forth. Three types of formative evaluation at the elementary level are widely used: the individual conference, the small-group conference, and peer conferencing.

The Individual Conference

The individual conference can occur informally at the student's desk or it can take place at a scheduled time. In the early stages of the writing process, responses and questions should be about writing ideas, content, audience, purpose, generating details, and so on. Questions should be open-ended. This gives the writer "space" to talk. When a writer is talking, he or she is thinking, clarifying, and making decisions. Teachers don't have to solve all writing problems for their students, but they can ask questions and suggest possible solutions.

In the editing and proofreading stage, a teacher might ask, "Why do you need a period here?" Students should try to answer the questions and add the correct punctuation marks. With the inexperienced writer, it's best not to mark all errors. Simply draw a double line to indicate where you stopped editing or proofreading the student's work. An individual conference can also be student directed if he or she finishes a draft, identifies a problem, or wants to share a revision or improvement of some type.

"Teachers need to look at each individual writer, and what's more, each writer will demonstrate different writing behaviors with different writing tasks."
—Jo-Ann Parry and David Hornsby
Write On: A Conference Approach to Writing

The Small-Group Conference

The small-group conference may consist of groups of three to five students who are at the same stage in the writing process or who are involved in the same type of writing project. The twofold goal of a small-group conference is to help students improve their own writing while also becoming writing evaluators for others. Minilessons work well in small-group conferences.

Consider holding a publisher's meeting during small-group conferences so students can help one another select writing to be published. Your role is to help students reach informed conclusions about their writing. For more information about this type of evaluation, see "Publishing Your Writing," in "The Process of Writing" section of this guide.

Peer Conferencing

Students also need to learn how to conference with others without the help of a teacher. We suggest that students work in pairs at first and use some type of checklist or guide when they conference. Always model how to use the checklist before you have students work on their own. Impose a time limit for peer-responding sessions to keep students on task (10-15 minutes).

To help your students prepare for peer-conferencing sessions, read "Writing Conferences" with the class (pages 38-39) in *Write Away*. Also refer to the basic unit for this chapter located in "The Process of Writing" section of this guide.

One easy method of peer responding is to ask a student to read his or her partner's paper and then generate several questions beginning with *who, what, where, when, why,* or *how*. The questions and paper are returned to the writer, who then responds to the questions. These questions serve as starting points for discussion. Students could also use one of the conferencing sheets provided at the end of this section. (See pages 141-142.)

Summative Evaluation

Students need to understand and value the writing process as much as the final product. Their focus should be on personal goals, not grades. However, grades must be assigned to at least some of their completed work. This is when summative evaluation is important. The following general principles will help you evaluate finished written products.

1. Clearly establish the criteria for evaluating each written selection. Limit the criteria so you do not overwhelm the students or yourself.

2. Ask students to help you develop the criteria. This can be done in individual conferences or with the entire class. Students readily accept and understand criteria they have helped develop.

3. Offer students ample opportunities for formative evaluation before giving their final products grades. Remember that students deserve credit for the work they have done during the writing process.

4. Attend first to overall content, focus, organization, and details during summative evaluation. Correctness and neatness are also important, but they are only part of the complete writing picture.

5. Involve your students in summative evaluation. You can do this by providing them with a form that helps them to identify the best parts of their writing, list the problems they encountered, and correct the parts they would revise if they had more time. Students should also share how much time they put into a project.

Approaches for Summative Evaluations

Holistic grading is a process used for evaluating a writing selection. The most basic approach to holistic grading is to read the paper rather quickly for a general impression. The paper is graded according to predetermined criteria matched to a scaled score called a "rubric." A reader might also compare a particular piece with several written selections already graded.

Teachers can use a basic rubric (scaled score) like the one that follows to rate the effectiveness of a piece of writing.

WRITING RUBRIC

4—EXCELLENT

Writing is . . .
- focused on the topic
- well organized (beginning, middle, end)
- detailed with precise word choice
- punctuated, spelled, capitalized correctly

3—GOOD

Writing is . . .
- generally focused on the topic
- adequately organized (beginning, middle, end)
- detailed with adequate word choice
- punctuated, spelled, capitalized adequately

2—FAIR

Writing is . . .
- loosely focused on the topic
- poorly organized (beginning, middle, end)
- inadequately detailed with limited word choice
- punctuated, spelled, and capitalized inadequately

1—WEAK

Writing is . . .
- not focused on the topic
- not organized (beginning, middle, end)
- not detailed with inadequate word choice
- punctuated, spelled, and capitalized incorrectly

Task-specific scoring accords a grade based on how well a student has accomplished specific rhetorical tasks. A teacher might, for example, create a scoring checklist or guide for a short fiction writing assignment. This checklist would include those elements that are inherent in this writing form—plot, characterization, point of view, and so on. Students must understand the criteria for scoring before they begin their writing.

Portfolio grading gives students an opportunity to be involved in the evaluation process. (See the next two pages for more information about portfolio assessment.)

A **performance system** is a quick and simple method of evaluation. A performance system is based on how a student applies what is learned. If students complete a writing activity, and it meets the previously established level of acceptability, they receive the preestablished grade or points for completing the assignment.

Using Writing Portfolios

More and more, teachers are using portfolios as an important part of their writing programs. Will portfolios be beneficial for you? Will they help you and your students assess their writing? Read on to find out.

What is a classroom portfolio?

A classroom portfolio is a representative sampling of a student's writing for evaluation. It differs from the traditional writing folder that contains all of a student's work.

Why should I ask students to compile classroom portfolios?

Students are directly involved in the assessment process as they go about choosing which pieces to include in their portfolios. Compiling portfolios also encourages students to monitor their own writing progress. They learn firsthand that writing is an involved, recursive process of writing and rewriting.

Teachers can utilize any or all methods of assessment when portfolios are used, including self-evaluation, peer evaluation, contract writing, and traditional grading.

How many writing samples should be included in a portfolio?

You and your students should make that decision. However, as a guide, ask your students to collect at least three pieces of writing in a portfolio each quarter. (Some teachers have their students contract for a specific amount of required writing.) All drafts for each written selection should be included. Usually, students are also required to include a reflective piece or self-critique sheet that assesses their writing progress.

Note: Some teachers want students to include in their portfolios one or two writing selections from other subject areas.

When do portfolios work best?

Students need blocks of class time to work on writing if they are going to produce effective portfolios. If portfolios are used correctly, beginning writers become practicing writers. Portfolios are excellent teaching tools for classrooms that incorporate writing workshops.

How can I help my students with their portfolio writing?

Provide your students with many opportunities to discuss their writing with each other. Make sharing sessions an important part of your class. Expect your students to evaluate their own writing and the writing of their peers—and help them to do so. Also be available to guide students when they need help with their writing. (Again, the handbook provides plenty of writing guidelines.) Finally, create a stimulating classroom environment that encourages students to immerse themselves in writing.

How do I evaluate/grade a portfolio?

Base each grade on the goals you and your students established at the beginning of the grading period, looking to the portfolio pieces for evidence of the achieved goals. Many teachers develop a critique sheet for assessment that is based on the goals established by the class. (It's very important that students know how many writing products they should include in their portfolios, how their written work should be arranged in their portfolios, and how the portfolios will be assessed.)

Note: See page 143 in this section for a copymaster that could prove helpful when evaluating portfolios.

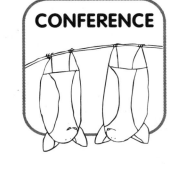

CONFERENCE

Conference Tips

DIRECTIONS: On the top half of this paper, list the things you really like about your partner's writing. On the bottom half, list the questions or suggestions you may have.

Author _____ **Date** _____

Title _____

What I Like

_____

_____

_____

_____

My Questions and Suggestions

_____

_____

_____

_____

CONFERENCE

Conference Checklist

DIRECTIONS: Answer these questions about your partner's nonfiction writing. (Write your ideas and suggestions on the back of this sheet.)

Author _____ Date _____

Title _____

Focus:

_____ Does the writing stay on the topic?

Organization:

_____ Does the writing have a beginning, a middle, and an ending?

Details:

_____ Are there details and examples about the subject?

Mechanics:

_____ Are the sentences easy to read?

_____ Are all the words spelled correctly?

_____ Does each sentence end with a punctuation mark?

_____ Are capital letters used where they are needed?

Name _____

Thinking About My Writing

THINK

I chose to publish this writing,
or put it in my portfolio, because _____

_____

_____

_____

As I wrote this paper, I learned _____

_____

_____

My conference partner
gave me these suggestions: _____

_____

_____

The next time I write, I would like to _____

_____

_____

Teacher's signature _____ **Date** _____

Reading-Writing CONNECTION

In this section, you will find lists of important, high-interest titles that relate to many chapters in *Write Away*. These lists will prove invaluable when planning extended units for these chapters. Remember to check the reading-level symbols. Titles without symbols are in the second-grade range.

Reading Levels:

E = Easy

C = Challenging

Keeping an Idea Notebook

The Chalk Doll
by Charlotte Pomerantz, 1989

The Day of Ahmed's Secret
by Florence Parry Heide, 1990

Frog and Toad Together
by Arnold Lobel, 1972

How to Get Famous in Brooklyn
by Amy Hest, 1995

I'm in Charge of Celebrations (C)
by Byrd Baylor, 1986

Knots on a Counting Rope
by Bill Martin and
John Archambault, 1966

My Family Vacation (C)
by Dayal Khalsa, 1988

My Grandmother's Cookie Jar
by Montzalee Miller, 1987

Owl Moon
by Jane Yolen, 1987

Soup (C)
by Robert Newton Peck, 1974

When I Was Young in the Mountains
by Cynthia Rylant, 1982

Writing in Journals

A Book of Your Own: (C)
Keeping a Diary or Journal
by Carla Stevens, 1993

Celia's Island Journal
by Celia Thaxter
(adapted by Loretta Krupinski), 1992

I Love Saturday
by Patricia Reilly Giff, 1991

Only Opal: The Diary of a Young Girl
by Jane Boulton and
Opal Whiteley, 1994

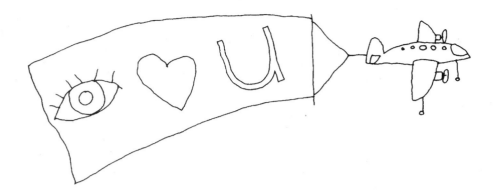

Writing Friendly Notes

Arthur's Birthday
by Marc Brown, 1989

Amelia Bedelia
by Peggy Parish, 1963

Amelia Bedelia and the Baby
by Peggy Parish, 1981

Good Work, Amelia Bedelia
by Peggy Parish, 1976

**Nate the Great and
the Lost List**
by Marjorie Weinman Sharmat, 1975

**Nate the Great and
the Missing Key**
by Marjorie Weinman Sharmat, 1981

**Nate the Great and
the Pillowcase**
by Marjorie Weinman Sharmat, 1993

**Nate the Great and
the Tardy Tortoise**
by Marjorie Weinman Sharmat, 1995

Writing Friendly Letters

Dear Brother
by Frank Asch, 1992

Don't Forget to Write
by Martina Selway, 1992

The Jolly Christmas Postman
by Janet and Allan Ahlberg, 1986

The Jolly Postman
by Janet and Allan Ahlberg, 1991

Kate Heads West
by Pat Brisson, 1990

A Letter to Amy
by Ezra Jack Keats, 1968

Your Best Friend, Kate
by Pat Brisson, 1989

Writing All-About-Me Stories

Abuela
by Arthur Dorros, 1991

**Aunt Elaine Does the Dance
from Spain**
by Leah Komaiko, 1992

Bigmama's
by Donald Crews, 1991

A Birthday Basket for Tia
by Pat Mora, 1992

Family Pictures
by Carmen Lomas Garza, 1990

Friday Night Is Papa Night
by Ruth A. Sonneborn, 1970

Fun/No Fun
by James Stevenson, 1996

Higher on the Door
by James Stevenson, 1987

I Want a Dog
by Dayal Khalsa, 1987

July
by James Stevenson, 1990

My Grandpa and the Sea
by Katherine Orr, 1990

Rumble, Thumble, Boom!
by Anna Grossnickle Hines, 1992

Thunder Cake
by Patricia Pollaco, 1990

Visit to Oma
by Marisabina Russo, 1991

When I Was Nine
by James Stevenson, 1986

Making Counting Books

Anno's Counting Book
by Mitsumasa Anno, 1977

Count-a-Saurus
by Nancy Blumenthal, 1989

A Dozen Dizzy Dogs
by William Hooks, 1990

Emeka's Gift:
An African Counting Story
by Ifeoma Onyefulu, 1995

I Spy Two Eyes:
Numbers in Art
by Jim Aylesworth, 1988

Moon Jump: a Cowntdown
by Paula Brown, 1993

Numbers (C)
by Suse MacDonald
and Bill Oakes, 1988

One Bear with Bees in His Hair
by Jakki Wood, 1990

One Crow:
A Counting Rhyme
by Jim Aylesworth, 1988

One Good Horse:
A Cowpuncher's Counting Book
by Ann Scott, 1990

One Gorilla
by Atsuko Morozumi, 1990

Sea Squares (C)
by Joy Hulme, 1991

Ten Black Dots
by Donald Crews, 1986

Ten Ways to Count to Ten: (C)
A Liberian Folktale
retold by Ruby Dee, 1988

The 12 Circus Rings
by Seymour Chwast, 1993

12 Ways to Get to 11
by Eve Merriam, 1993

The Wildlife 1*2*3
by Jan Thornhill, 1989

one spot
two spots
old spot
new spots

Writing News Stories

Deadline!: From News to Newspaper
by Gail Gibbons, 1987

**The Furry News:
How to Make a Newspaper**
by Loreen Leedy, 1990

**What's It Like to Be a
Newspaper Reporter?** Ⓒ
by Janet Craig, 1990

Writing Directions

**Better Homes and
Gardens at the Zoo**
by Better Homes and
Gardens, Inc., 1989

**The Children's Step-By-Step
Cook Book: Photographic
Cooking Lessons for
Young Chefs** Ⓒ
by Angela Wilkes, 1994

Everybody Cooks Rice
by Norah Dooley, 1992

**From Pictures to Words:
A Book About Making a Book** Ⓒ
by Janet Stevens, 1995

**The Kids' Multicultural Cookbook:
Food and Fun Around the World**
by Deanna F. Cook, 1995

**Mudworks: Creative Clay, Dough,
and Modeling Experiences**
by MaryAnn F. Kohl, 1989

**Planes and Other
Flying Things**
by Florence Temko, 1995

Sewing by Hand
by Christine Hoffman, 1994

Writing Reports

Animal Fact/Animal Fable
by Seymour Simon, 1979

Beacons of Light: Lighthouses
by Gail Gibbons, 1990

A Chick Hatches
by Joanna Cole, 1976

Creepy, Crawly, Caterpillars
by Margery Facklam, 1996

Dinosaur Story
by Joanna Cole, 1974

Dinosaurs Are Different
by Aliki, 1985

**Dorling Kindersley
Children's Illustrated Dictionary**
by John McIlwain, 1994

A Flower Grows
by Ken Robbins, 1990

Hungry, Hungry Sharks
by Joanna Cole, 1986

Jaguar in the Rain Forest
by Joanne Ryder, 1996

**The Magic School Bus:
Inside the Earth**
by Joanna Cole, 1987

An Octopus Is Amazing
by Patricia Lauber, 1990

**OGBO: Sharing Life in an African
Village**
by Ifeoma Onyefulu, 1996

Pond Year
by Mike Bostock, 1995

**The Post Office Book:
Mail and How It Moves**
by Gail Gibbons, 1982

Rain Forest Babies
by Kathy Darling, 1996

**Stories on Stone: Rock Art/Images
from the Ancient Ones**
by Jennifer Owens Dewey, 1996

**Timber! From Trees
to Word Products**
by William Jaspersohn, 1996

Volcanoes
by Jenny Wood, 1990

Wildfires
by Seymour Simon, 1996

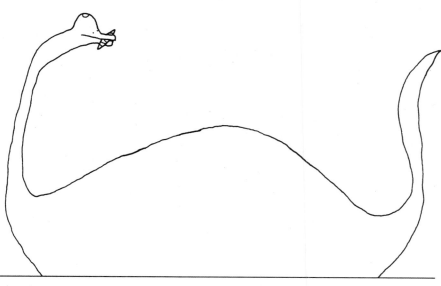

Making Picture Dictionaries

C Is for Curious: An ABC of Feelings
by Woodleigh Hubbard, 1990

City Seen from A to Z
by Rachel Isadora, 1992

Funny Side Up
by Mike Thaler, 1985

**Mi primer libro de palabras
en Español**
by Angela Wilkes and Rubi Borgia, 1993

**Mon Primier Livre de Mots
en Francais**
by Angela Wilkes and Annie Heminway,
1993

**Q Is for Duck:
An Alphabet Guessing Book**
by Mary Elting and Michael Folsom,
1980

Writing Circle Stories

The Amazing Bone
by William Steig, 1976

The Funny Little Woman
by Arlene Mosel, 1972

If You Give a Moose a Muffin
by Laura Joffe Numeroff, 1991

If You Give a Mouse a Cookie
by Laura Joffe Numeroff, 1985

Let the Lynx Come In
by Jonathan London, 1996

Millions of Cats
by Wanda Gag, 1977

Moon Tiger
by Phyllis Root, 1988

The Red Racer
by Audrey Wood, 1996

Rosie's Walk
by Pat Hutchins, 1986

Sleep Out
by Carol and Donald Carrick, 1982

Sylvester and the Magic Pebble
by William Steig, 1969

The Tale of Peter Rabbit
by Beatrix Potter, 1903

Where the Wild Things Are
by Maurice Sendak, 1963

Why a Disguise?
by Laura Joffe Numeroff, 1996

Writing Add-On Stories

Dogs Don't Wear Sneakers
by Laura Joffe Numeroff, 1993

Drummer Hoff
adapted by Barbara Emberely, 1984

The Gingerbread Boy
by Paul Galdone, 1985

The Great Big Enormous Turnip
by Alexei Tolstoy and
Helen Oxenbury, 1983

A Guest Is a Guest
by John Himmelman, 1991

I Know an Old Lady
by Rose Bonne, 1985

Is Your Mama a Llama? (E)
by Deborah Gaurino, 1989

The Little Red Hen
by Paul Galdone, 1985

Mr. Gumpy's Outing
by John Burningham, 1984

Mrs. Wishy Washy (E)
by Joy Cowley, 1987

Ms. MacDonald Has a Class
by Jan Ormerod, 1996

My Very Own Octopus
by Bernard Most, 1991

The Napping House (E)
by Audrey Wood, 1984

Over in the Meadow
by John Langstaff, 1973

Polar Bear, Polar Bear, (E)
What Do You Hear?
by Bill Martin, Jr., 1991

The Runaway Bunny
by Margaret Wise Brown, 1972

Stone Soup
by Ann McGovern, 1986

Wave Goodbye (E)
by Rob Reid, 1961

Writing Fables

Aesop's Fables
  by Russell Ash, 1990

Aesop's Fables
  by Heidi Holder, 1993

Aesop's Fables
  by Ann McGovern, 1963

Aesop's Fables
  by Tom Paxton, 1988

**Androcles and the Lion,
and Other Aesop's Fables**
  by Tom Paxton, 1991

Anno's Aesop
  by Mitsumasa Anno, 1989

**Belling the Cat, and
Other Aesop's Fables**
  by Tom Paxton, 1990

The Best of Aesop's Fables
  by Margaret Clark, 1990

The Children's Aesop
  by Robert Byrd, 1992

**The City Mouse and
the Country Mouse**
  by Jody Wheeler, 1985

Fables
  by Arnold Lobel, 1980

**Feathers and Tails: Animal Fables
from Around the World**
  by David Kheridian, 1992

The Monkey and the Crocodile
  by Paul Galdone, 1969

Old Man Whickutt's Donkey
  by Mary Calhoun, 1975

Once a Mouse
  by Marcia Brown, 1961

**Once Upon Another: The Tortoise
and the Hare**
  retold by Suse MacDonald
  and Bill Oakes, 1990

Seven Blind Mice
  by Ed Young, 1992

**Three Rolls and One Doughnut:
Fables from Russia**
  by Mirra Ginsburg, 1970

**The Town Mouse and the
Country Mouse**
  by Helen Craig, 1992

Town Mouse, Country Mouse
  by Jan Brett, 1994

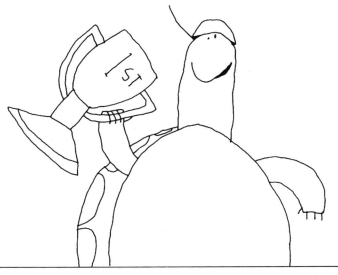

Writing Mysteries

The ABC Mystery
by Doug Cushman, 1993

Cam Jansen and the Chocolate Fudge Mystery
by David Adler, 1993

Cam Jansen and the Mystery at the Monkey House
by David Adler, 1985

Cam Jansen and the Mystery of the Television Dog
by David Adler, 1981

The Case of the Anteater's Missing Lunch
by Vivian Binnamin, 1990

The Case of the Cat's Meow
by Crosby Bonsall, 1965

The Case of the Cool Itch Kids
by Patricia Reilly Giff, 1989

The Case of the Scaredy Cats
by Crosby Bonsall, 1971

The Case of the Secret Message Ⓒ
by Parker C. Hinter, 1994

Flatfoot Fox and the Case of the Bashful Beaver
by Eth Clifford, 1995

Gertrude, the Bulldog Detective
by Eileen Christelow, 1992

Hot Fudge
by James Howe, 1990

Nate the Great and the Boring Beach Bag
by Marjorie Weinman Sharmat, 1987

Nate the Great and the Fishy Prize
by Marjorie Weinman Sharmat, 1985

Private I. Guana: The Case of the Missing Chameleon
by Nina Laden, 1995

The Rooftop Mystery
by Joan Lexau, 1968

The Seven Treasure Hunts Ⓒ
by Betsy Byars, 1991

Sly P.I.: The Case of the Missing Shoes
by Cathy Stefanec-Ogren, 1989

The Thieves of Peck's Pocket
by Teryl Euvremer, 1990

Writing Small Poems

All Small: Poems
by David McCord, 1986

all the small poems
by David McCord, 1986

A Helpful Alphabet of Friendly Objects
by John Updike, 1995

Sea Watch
by Jane Yolen, 1996

Sing to the Sun
by Bryan Ashley, 1992

A Suitcase of Seaweed and Other Poems
by Janet S. Wong, 1996

Through Our Eyes: Poems and Pictures About Growing Up
selected by Lee Bennett Hopkins, 1992

Making Shape Poems

Any Me I Want to Be
by Karla Kuskin, 1972

Creepy Crawly Critters and Other Halloween Tongue Twisters
by Nolla Buck, 1995

Doodle Dandies
by J. Patrick Lewis (scheduled for 1998)

A Hippopotamusn't and Other Animal Verses
by J. Patrick Lewis, 1990

If I Had a Paka: Poems in Eleven Languages
by Charlotte Pomerantz, 1993

Jeremy Kooloo
by Tim Mahurin, 1995

Sing a Song of Popcorn: Every Child's Book of Poems
edited by Beatrice S. DeRegniers, 1988

Sunflakes: Poems for Children
edited by Lillian Moore, 1992

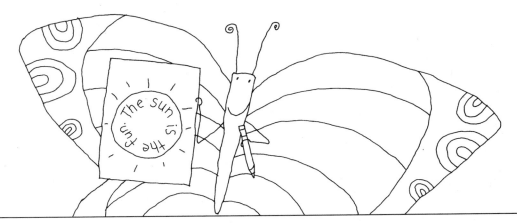

Reading Graphics

Bicycle Book
by Gail Gibbons, 1990

Cars and How They Go
by Joanna Cole, 1983

Cars and Trucks and Things That Go
by Richard Scarry, 1974

How a House Is Built
by Gail Gibbons, 1990

Monarch Butterfly
by Gail Gibbons, 1989

Pretend Soup and Other Real Recipes
by Molly Katzen
and Ann Henderson, 1994

Richard Scarry's Best Busy Year Ever
by Richard Scarry, 1991

Richard Scarry's What Do People Do All Day?
by Richard Scarry, 1968

Tunnels
by Gail Gibbons, 1984

Performing Stories

The Almost Awful Play
by Patricia Reilly Giff, 1985

Lights, Action, Land-Ho!
by Judy Delton, 1992

Show Time at the Polk Street School: Plays You Can Do Yourself or in the Classroom
by Patricia Reilly Giff, 1992

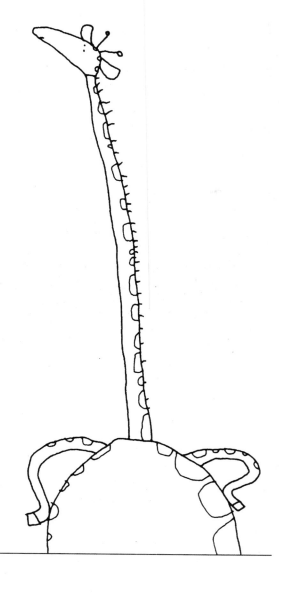

Telling Stories

The Adventures of Spider
by Joyce Cooper Arkhurst, 1964

Aunt Isabel Tells a Good One
by Kate Duke, 1992

**Front Porch Stories at
the One-Room School**
by Eleanora E. Tate, 1992

Grandfather Tang's Story
by Ann Tompert, 1990

More Stories Julian Tells C
by Ann Cameron, 1986

**Princess Bee and the Royal
Good-Night Story**
by Sandy Asher, 1990

The Stories Julian Tells C
by Ann Cameron, 1981

Three by the Sea
by Edward Marshall, 1981

Chapter Books/Series

Amelia Bedelia books
by Peggy Parrish

Cam Jensen books
by David Adler

Commander Toad books
by Jane Yolen

Fourth Floor Twins books
by David Adler

Frog and Toad books
by Arnold Lobel

Henry and Mudge books
by Cynthia Rylant

Horrible Harry books
by Suzy Kline

Jenny Archer books
by Ellen Conford

M & M books
by Pat Ross

Magic School Bus books
by Joanna Cole

Ramona books C
by Beverly Cleary

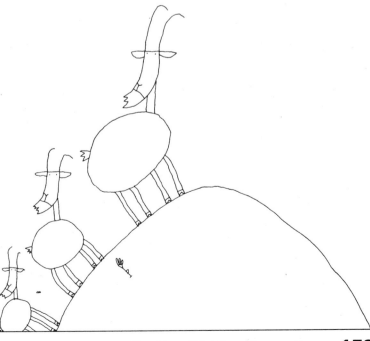

BIBLIOGRAPHY

The resources in this bibliography are helpful titles teachers may consult for additional information related to each handbook section.

THE PROCESS OF WRITING

ALL ABOUT WRITING

Calkins, Lucy McCormick. *Living Between the Lines*. Portsmouth: Heinemann, 1991.

Christelow, Eileen. *What Do Authors Do?* New York: Clarion, 1995.

Fraser, Jane, and Donna Skolnick. *On Their Way: Celebrating Second Graders as They Read and Write*. Portsmouth: Heinemann, 1994.

Graves, Donald H. *A Fresh Look at Writing*. Portsmouth: Heinemann, 1994.

Lensmire, Timothy J. *When Children Write*. New York: Teacher's College Press, 1994.

Lloyd, Pamela. *How Writers Write*. Portsmouth: Heinemann, 1987.

Millett, Nancy. *Teaching the Writing Process*. Boston: Houghton Mifflin, 1986.

Moffett, James, and Betty Wagner. *Student-Centered Language Arts, K-12*. Portsmouth: Heinemann, 1992.

Murray, Donald. *Learning by Teaching*. Upper Montclair: Boynton Cook, 1982.

Routman, Regie. *Literacy at the Crossroads*. Portsmouth: Heinemann, 1996.

Tompkins, Gail E. *Teaching Writing*. New York: Macmillan College Publishing Company, 1993.

PREWRITING AND DRAFTING

Bumgardner, Joyce C. *My Writing Book*. New York: Scholastic, 1989.

Graves, Donald. *Investigate Nonfiction*. Portsmouth: Heinemann, 1989.

Harwayne, Shelley. *Lasting Impressions: Weaving Literature into the Writing Workshop*. Portsmouth: Heinemann, 1992.

Jett-Simpson, Mary, and Lauren Leslie. "Writing Development." *Ecological Assessment*. Schofield, WI: Wisconsin State Reading Association, 1994.

Kovacs, Deborah, and James Prowler. *Meet the Authors and Illustrators: 60 Creators of Favorite Children's Books Talk About Their Work*. New York: Scholastic, 1991.

Rico, Gabriel L. *Writing the Natural Way: Using Right-Brain Techniques to Release Your Expressive Powers*. Los Angeles: Tarcher, 1983.

REVISING AND CHECKING

Calkins, Lucy McCormick. *The Art of Teaching Writing*. Portsmouth: Heinemann, 1994.

Fairfax, Barbara, and Adela Garcia. *Read! Write! Publish! Making Books in the Classroom Grades 1-5*. Cypress, CA: Creative Teaching Press, 1992.

Fletcher, Ralph. *What a Writer Needs*. Portsmouth: Heinemann, 1993.

Johnson, Paul. *Literacy Through the Book Arts*. Portsmouth: Heinemann, 1993.

Nathan, Ruth, et al. *Classroom Strategies That Work: An Elementary Teacher's Guide to Process Writing*. Portsmouth: Heinemann, 1989.

Ross, Elinor Parry. *The Workshop Approach: A Framework for Literacy*. Norwood, MA: Christopher-Gordon Publishers, Inc., 1996.

Smith, Jennifer. "Periodicals That Publish Children's Original Work." *Language Arts* 65.2 (1988).

SENTENCES AND PARAGRAPHS

Moffet, James. *Active Voices I*. Upper Montclair: Boynton Cook, 1987.

Petty, Walter T., Dorothy C. Petty, and Richard T. Salzer. "Supporting the Writing Process." *Experiences in Language*. Boston: Allyn and Bacon, 1994.

Strong, William. *Sentence Combining and Paragraph Building*. New York: McGraw, 1981.

THE FORMS OF WRITING

PERSONAL WRITING

Barkin, Carol, and Elizabeth James. *Sincerely Yours: How to Write Great Letters*. New York: Clarion, 1993.

Buchman, Dian D. *Family Fill-In Book: Discovering Your Roots*. New York: Scholastic, 1994.

Free Stuff for Kids. Deephaven, MN: Meadowbrook, 1995.

Fulwiler, Toby, ed. *The Journal Book*. Portsmouth: Heinemann, 1987.

Harwayne, Shelly. *Lasting Impressions: Weaving Literature into the Writing Workshop*. Portsmouth: Heinemann, 1992.

Kaye, Peggy. "Write a Letter." *Games for Writing*. New York: Farrar, Straus & Giroux, 1995.

Ohanian, Susan. *Who's in Charge? A Teacher Speaks Her Mind*. Portsmouth: Heinemann, 1994.

Stevens, Carla. *A Book of Your Own: Keeping a Diary or Journal*. New York: Clarion Books, 1993.

Stillman, Peter. *Families Writing*. Cincinnati: Writer's Digest Books, 1989.

Wollman-Bonilla, Julie. *Response Journals: Inviting Students to Think and Write about Literature*. New York: Scholastic, 1991.

SUBJECT WRITING

Aliki. *How a Book is Made*. New York: Crowell, 1986.

Barchers, Suzanne I. *Creating and Managing the Literate Classroom*. Englewood, CO: Libraries Unlimited, 1990.

Clark, Roy Peter. *Free to Write: A Journalist Teaches Young Writers*. Portsmouth: Heinemann, 1987.

D'Arcy, Pat. *Making Sense, Shaping Meaning*. Portsmouth: Heinemann, 1989.

Guthrie, Donna, Nancy Bentley, and Katy Keck Arnsteen. *The Young Author's Do-It-Yourself Book: How to Write, Illustrate, and Produce Your Own Book*. Brookfield, CT: The Millbrook Press, 1994.

Ohanian, Susan. "Across the Curriculum from A to Z." *Learning* 18.2 (1987).

RESEARCH WRITING

Bunting, Jane. *The Children's Visual Dictionary*. London: Dorling Kindersley, 1995.

Doris, Ellen. *Doing What Scientists Do: Children Learn to Investigate Their World*. Portsmouth: Heinemann, 1991.

Gamberg, R., et al. *Learning and Loving It: Theme Studies in the Classroom*. Portsmouth: Heinemann, 1988.

Hansen, Jane. "Content Areas." *When Writers Read*. Portsmouth: Heinemann, 1995.

James, Elizabeth, and Carol Barkin. *How to Write a Great School Report*. New York: Beach Tree Books, 1983.

Kobrin, Beverly. *Eyeopeners II*. New York: Scholastic, 1995.

McIlwain, John. *The Dorling Kindersley Children's Illustrated Dictionary*. London: Dorling Kindersley, 1994.

Ostrow, Jull. *A Room with a Different View: First Through Third Graders Build Community and Create Curriculum*. York, ME: Stenhouse, 1995.

Scarry, Richard. *Richard Scarry's Best Word Book Ever*. New York: Golden Press, 1963.

Sorenson, Marilou, and Barbara Lehman. *Teaching with Children's Books*. Urbana, IL: NCTE, 1995.

Ward, Geoff. *I've Got a Project On . . . .* Portsmouth: Heinemann, 1988.

Williams, Bare. *The Internet for Teachers*. Foster City, CA: IDG Books Worldwide, Inc., 1995.

STORY WRITING

Bader, Barbara. *Aesop & Company*. Boston: Houghton Mifflin, 1991.

Deen, Rosemary, and Marie Ponsot. *The Common Sense: What to Write, How to Write It, and Why*. Portsmouth: Heinemann, 1985.

Graves, Donald. *Experiment with Fiction*. Portsmouth: Heinemann, 1989.

Howe, James. "Writing Mysteries for Children." *The Horn Book* Mar.-Apr. 1990.

Johnson, Terry, and Daphne Louis. *Bringing It All Together: A Program for Literacy*. Portsmouth: Heinemann, 1990.

Moir, Hughes, Melissa Cain, and Leslie Prosak-Beres. *Collected Perspectives: Choosing and Using Books for the Classroom*. Boston: Christopher-Gordon, 1992.

Robb, Laura. *Whole Language, Whole Learners: Creating a Literature-Centered Curriculum*. New York: Quill/William Morrow, 1995.

POETRY WRITING

Chatton, Barbara. *Using Poetry Across the Curriculum: A Whole Language Approach*. Phoenix: Oryx Press, 1993.

Cullinan, Bernice, et al. *Three Voices: An Invitation to Poetry Across the Curriculum*. York, ME: Stenhouse, 1995.

Janeczko, Paul. *Poetry from A to Z*. New York: Bradbury Press, 1994.

Livingston, Myra Cohn. *Poem-Making: Ways to Begin Writing Poetry*. New York: Harper Collins, 1991.

Oliver, Mary. *A Poetry Handbook*. New York: Harcourt Brace and Co., 1994.

Steinbergh, Judith. *Reading and Writing Poetry: A Guidebook for Teachers*. New York: Scholastic, 1994.

Williams, Miller. *Patterns of Poetry*. Baton Rouge: Louisiana State University Press, 1986.

THE TOOLS OF LEARNING

READING SKILLS/WORKING WITH WORDS

Allington, Richard L., and Patricia M. Cunningham. *Schools That Work: Where All Children Read and Write*. New York: HarperCollins, 1996.

Bear, Donald, et al. *Words Their Way: Word Study for Phonics, Vocabulary, and Spelling Instruction*. Englewood Cliffs: Merrill/Prentice-Hall, 1995.

Brinkerhoff, Stevie Auld. *Linking: Developing Strategic Readers and Writers in the Primary Classroom*. Grand Rapids, MI: Michigan Reading Association, 1993.

Cullinan, Bernice, ed. *Invitation to Read: More Children's Literature in the Reading Program*. Newark: International Reading Association, 1992.

Cunningham, Patricia. *Phonics They Use: Words for Reading and Writing*. 2nd ed. New York: HarperCollins, 1995.

Green, Joseph. *The Word Wall: Teaching Vocabulary Through Immersion*. Portsmouth: Heinemann, 1993.

Moline, Steve. *I See What You Mean: Children at Work with Visual Information*. York, ME: Stenhouse, 1995.

Mooney, Margaret E. *Reading to, with, and by Children*. Katonah, NY: Richard C. Owen, 1990.

Morris, Darrell. "The Relationship Between Children's Concept of Word in Text and Phoneme Awareness in Learning to Read: A Longitudinal Study." *Research in the Teaching of English* 27.2 (1993).

Ogle, Donna. "KWL: A Teaching Model That Develops Active Reading of Expository Text." *The Reading Teacher* 39.1 (1986).

Peterson, Ralph, and Maryann Eeds. *Grand Conversations: Literature Groups in Action*. New York: Scholastic, 1990.

Powell, Debbie, and David Hornsby. *Learning Phonics and Spelling in a Whole Language Classroom*. New York: Scholastic, 1993.

Steed, Robin. *Touchphonics*. Northbeach, CA: Touchphonics Reading Systems, 1993.

Young, Sue. *The Rhyming Dictionary*. New York: Scholastic, 1994.

SPEAKING AND LISTENING SKILLS

Barchers, Suzanne I. *Teaching Language Arts: An Integrated Approach*. St. Paul: West Publishing, 1994.

Beaty, Janice J. *Picture Book Storytelling: Literature Activities for Young Children*. Fort Worth: Harcourt Brace, 1994.

Hamilton, Martha, and Mitch Weiss. *Children Tell Stories*. Katonah, NY: Richard C. Owen, 1990.

Hill, Susan. *Readers Theatre: Performing the Text*. Winnipeg, Manitoba: Peguis, 1992.

Kallevig, Christine Petrell. *Folding Stories: Storytelling and Origami Together As One*. Newburgh, IN: Storytime Ink International, 1991.

Kinghorn, Harriet R. *Every Child a Storyteller: A Handbook of Ideas*. Englewood, CO: Teacher Ideas Press, 1991.

Larrick, Nancy. *Let's Do a Poem! Introducing Poetry to Children*. New York: Delacorte Press, 1991.

Milford, Susan. *Tales Alive! Ten Multicultural Folktales with Activities*. Charlotte: Williamson Publishing, 1995.

Moffett, James, and Betty Wagner. *Student-Centered Language Arts, K-12*. Portsmouth: Heinemann, 1992.

Norton, Donna, and Saundra E. Norton. *Language Arts Activities for Children*. New York: Merrill, 1994.

Wolf, Allan. *It's Show Time: Poetry from the Page to the Stage*. Asheville, NC: Poetry Alive! Publications, 1993.

LEARNING SKILLS

Bayer, Ann Shea. *Collaborative-Apprenticeship Learning: Learning and Thinking Across the Curriculum, K-12*. Mountain View, CA: Mayfield, 1990.

Bromley, Karen, Linda Irwin-De Vitis, and Marcia Modlo. *Graphic Organizers*. New York: Scholastic, 1995.

Lee, Martin, and Marcia Miller. *Great Graphing*. New York: Scholastic, 1993.

Olson, Carol Booth. *Thinking Writing: Fostering Critical Thinking Through Writing*. New York: HarperCollins, 1992.

Short, Kathy G., Jerome C. Harste, and Carolyn Burke. *Creating Classrooms for Authors and Inquirers*. Portsmouth: Heinemann, 1996.

CHECKING YOUR SPELLING

Cramer, R. L., and J. Cipielewski. "Research in Action: A Study of Spelling Errors in 18,599 Written Compositions of Children in Grades 1-8." *Spelling Research and Information: An Overview of Current Research and Practices*. Glenview, IL: Scott, Foresman and Co., 1995.

Fry, E., D. Fountoukidis, and J. Polk. *The NEW Reading Teacher's Book of Lists*. Englewood Cliffs: Prentice Hall, 1985.

Gentry, J. Richard. *Spel . . . Is a Four-Letter Word*. Portsmouth: Heinemann, 1987.

Greenbaum, C. R. *Spellmaster*. Austin: Pro-Ed, 1987.

Henderson, Edmund. *Teaching Spelling*. Boston: Houghton Mifflin, 1985.

Hillerich, Robert. *A Writing Vocabulary for Elementary Children*. Springfield, IL: Charles Thomas, 1978.

Moats, Louisa Cook. *Spelling: Development, Disability, and Instruction*. Baltimore: York Press, 1995.

Moore, George, Richard A. Talbot, and G. Willard Woodruff. *Spellex: Word Finder*. Billerica, MA: Curriculum Associates, 1988.

Spelling Research and Information: An Overview of Current Research and Practices. Glenview, IL: Scott, Foresman and Co., 1995.

Wilde, Sandra. *You Kan Red This! Spelling and Punctuation for Whole Language Classrooms, K-6*. Portsmouth: Heinemann, 1992.

Woodruff, G. W., et al. *Working with Words in Spelling*. Lexington, MA: D.C. Heath, 1990.

THE STUDENT ALMANAC

THE STUDENT ALMANAC

Buckley, Susan, and Elspeth Leacock. *Hands-On Geography*. New York: Scholastic, 1993.

Carlisle, Madelyn Wood. *Marvelously Meaningful Maps*. Hauppauge, NY: Barron's, 1992.

Cyclopedia: The Portable Visual Encyclopedia. Philadelphia: Running Press, 1993.

Kipfer, Barbara Ann. *1,400 Things For Kids to be Happy About Book: The Happy Book*. New York: Workman, 1994.

Knowlton, Jack, and Harriet Barton. *Maps & Globes*. New York: HarperCollins, 1985.

Perham, Molly, and Philip Steele. *The Children's Illustrated World Atlas*. Philadelphia: Courage Books, 1992.

Taylor, Barbara. *Maps and Mapping*. New York: Kingfisher Books, 1993.

WORKING WITH MATH

Baker, Ann, and Johnny Baker. *Mathematics in Process*. Portsmouth: Heinemann, 1990.

Burns, Marilyn. *About Teaching Mathematics: A K-8 Resource*. New Rochelle: Math Solutions Publications, 1992.

HISTORY IN THE MAKING

Fry, Plantagenet Somerset. *The Dorling Kindersley History of the World*. New York: Dorling Kindersley, 1994.

Perez-Stable, Maria A., and Mary Hurlburt Cordier. *Understanding American History Through Children's Literature: Instructional Units and Activities for Grades K-8*. Phoenix, AZ: Oryx Press, 1994.

Tunnell, Michael, and Richard Ammon. *The Story of Ourselves: Teaching History Through Children's Literature*. Portsmouth: Heinemann, 1993.

EVALUATING/ASSESSING/MONITORING

Allington, Richard L., and Patricia M. Cunningham. *Schools That Work*. New York: HarperCollins, 1996.

Anthony, Robert, et al. *Evaluating Literacy: A Perspective for Change*. Portsmouth: Heinemann, 1991.

Cambourne, Brian. *The Whole Story: Natural Learning and the Acquisition of Literacy in the Classroom*. New York: Scholastic, 1989.

Davies, Anne, et al. *Together Is Better: Collaborative Assessment, Evaluation, and Reporting*. Manitoba: Peguis, 1992.

Graves, Donald H., and Bonnie S. Sunstein, eds. *Portfolio Portraits*. Portsmouth: Heinemann, 1992.

Harp, Bill, ed. *Assessment and Evaluation in Whole Language Programs*. Norwood, MA: Christopher-Gordon, 1991.

Jett-Simpson, Mary, and Lauren Leslie. *Ecological Assessment*. Schofield, WI: Wisconsin State Reading Association, 1994.

Rhodes, Lynn K., ed. *Literacy Assessment: A Handbook of Instruments*. Portsmouth: Heinemann, 1993.

Rhodes, Lynn K., and Nancy Shanklin. *Windows into Literacy: Assessing Learners, K-8*. Portsmouth: Heinemann, 1993.

Woodward, Helen. *Negotiated Evaluation: Involving Children and Parents in the Process*. Portsmouth: Heinemann, 1994.

READING/WRITING CONNECTION

Bishop, Rudine Sims, ed. *Kaleidoscope: A Multicultural Booklist for Grades K-8*. Urbana, IL: NCTE, 1994.

Cullinan, Bernice E. *Literature and the Child*. 2nd ed. San Diego: Harcourt Brace Jovanovich, 1989.

Danielson, Kathy Everts, and Jan LaBonty. *Integrating Reading and Writing Through Children's Literature*. Boston: Allyn and Bacon, 1993.

Hearne, Betsy. *Choosing Books for Children*. New York: Delacorte, 1990.

Jensen, Julie., and Nancy L. Roser, eds. *Adventuring with Books: A Booklist for Pre-K-Grade 6*. 10th ed. Urbana, IL: NCTE, 1993.

Johnson, Terry D., and Daphne R. Louis. *Bringing It All Together: A Program for Literacy*. Portsmouth: Heinemann, 1990.

Johnson, Terry D., and Daphne R. Louis. *Literacy Through Literature*. Portsmouth: Heinemann. Urbana, IL.

Kruse, Ginny Moore, and Kathleen T. Horning. *Multicultural Literature for Children and Young Adults*. 3rd ed. Madison, WI: University of Wisconsin Cooperative Children's Book Center, 1991.

Sharkey, Paulete Bochnig, and Jim Roginski, eds. *Newbery and Caldecott Medal and Honor Books in Other Media*. New York: Neal-Schuman Publishers, 1992.

Sutherland, Zena, and May Hill Arbuthnot. *Children and Books*. 8th ed. New York: HarperCollins, 1991.

Program OVERVIEW

This overview helps answer a very important question: What is the **Write Away Language Series** all about? Of special interest to you will be the introduction to the *Language Series* on page 176 and the overview of activities that follows on pages 177-180. This section concludes with an explanation of various program activities, from chapter notes to the two types of daily language sentences.

Introducing . . .

A Closer Look at . . .

Building a Writing and Language Program with the *Write Away Language Series*

The *Write Away Language Series* is a complete language and learning program for level 2. The program provides teachers with a rich resource of activities—including, among other things, extended writing units, basic language units, practice workshops, minilessons, and MUG Shot Sentences for daily language practice. Other sections provide practical guidelines for implementing the program.

What is included in the series?

The *Language Series* is packaged in a program kit containing three basic elements. These elements include . . .

Write Away **Student Handbook**—A hardcover copy of the handbook is included for handy teacher reference. (Each student must have access to a copy of the student handbook as well.)

Write Away **Student SourceBook**—Each kit includes one SourceBook, containing workshops, minilessons, and MUG Shot Sentences for teachers to reproduce and use in their classrooms. (Classroom sets of the SourceBooks may also be purchased.)

The *Program Guide*—This three-ring binder contains more than 500 pages of information, including chapter notes and activities that coordinate with the chapters in the *Write Away* handbook.

> **The overview charts on the next four pages identify the coordinating activities for each chapter in the student handbook.**

The PROCESS of Writing

All About Writing

Prewriting and Drafting

Revising and Checking

Sentences and Paragraphs

Basic units and extended units include chapter notes and, in most cases, reproducible blackline masters.

The FORMS of Writing

The TOOLS of Learning

Type of Activity

The Proofreader's GUIDE

The basic skills in this section are covered in Practice Workshops, Minilessons, and daily MUG Shot Sentences.

The Student ALMANAC

A Closer Look at
Chapter Notes

The unit chapter notes introduce you to each chapter in *Write Away* and provide implementation guidelines, special planning notes, and reproducible blackline masters for the units in the program.

Introductory Page ·····

Implementation Guidelines

Special Planning Notes ·····

(handbook pages 118-125)

Writing Reports

Classrooms where children are searching for information and reporting their findings are very exciting places. When they have the opportunity to choose topics of interest, do research, and then record what they have learned, children are onto something new and wonderful.

Writing Reports begins with an introduction about a boy intent on studying his favorite dinosaur. Young writers are then guided through an information search; helpful organizing ideas—note cards and gathering grids; instruction in writing the report; and a student model. The chapter ends with a list of alternatives to the traditional report format, and includes a model poem and story.

Rationale
- ✔ **Students need the opportunity to explore topics of interest.**
- ✔ **Children build research skills and begin to think critically as they select, organize, and share material in a written report.**

Major Concepts
- ✱ Selecting an interesting topic and asking questions about it is the first step in report writing. (pages 118-119)
- ✱ Note cards and gathering grids help students record and organize information. (pages 120-121)
- ✱ Reports have a beginning, a middle, and an ending—name the subject, share information, and give a brief review or personal response. (page 122)
- ✱ Pictures add meaning to reports. (page 123)
- ✱ There are many ways to report on information. (pages 124-125)

Planning Notes
Materials: Books and other resources about topics you are studying, time for library trips, large paper for grids, note cards, a large wall chart, blackline masters

Reading/Writing Connections: See "Special Planning Notes" at the end of this unit.

Early Literacy Connections: See "Special Planning Notes" at the end of this unit.

Technology Connections: See "Special Planning Notes" at the end of this unit.

Special Planning Notes

Minilessons

Ten Elephants or Twelve? . . . . **Conflicting Information**

READ the following example: "John read in one book that his dinosaur weighed as much as 10 elephants; another source said 12." **DISCUSS** what your students should do about conflicting information. **SUGGEST** looking at a third source. **TELL** children to compare copyright dates; the most recent source is usually more accurate. Sometimes children may write both "facts" and tell their readers that no one seems to know for sure.

Cover to Cover . . . . **Nonfiction Book Structure**

ASK every student to pick a favorite nonfiction book. **TURN** to page 117 in the student handbook, "Using Nonfiction Books," and **ASK** children to find the parts in their book.

Special Needs

Students who are not yet independent readers can gather information from sound filmstrips, CD's, and other multimedia resources. They can also use nonfiction books on tape if they are available.

Children who speak languages other than English will benefit from reading information in their first language, as well as in English. Titles in other languages are available from the Scholastic catalog (1-800-724-6527) and Bookman, Inc., (1-800-328-8411) at reduced cost to teachers.

Other Challenges **Writing Whole Books:** Report writing often motivates students to write whole nonfiction books. Writing whole books helps children develop their graphic skills, employing diagrams, graphs, and charts. Aliki's books and the books in *The Magic School Bus* series demonstrate the use of graphics. Also refer students to the handbook chapters "Reading Graphics" (pages 171-175) and "Using a Glossary" (pages 204-205).

Write to the Handbook

Getting Started (handbook pages 118 and 123)
- A written report is the final product of lots of information gathering. It is best done in conjunction with a thematic unit extended over a period of time (John Walker's class was studying dinosaurs). At this age children may do reports in small groups, with an older student in a "buddy project," or as an individual project.
- Introduce the process of report writing by reading aloud page 118 and then reading John Walker's report on page 123. Tell students they are going to learn how to gather information and write their own reports.

Finding Information for Reports (pages 119-121)
- Read the two sections on page 119 aloud. After you read each point, relate it to a specific topic—dinosaurs or a current topic of study. Then have students (as individuals or with their research "team") begin work on the blackline master "Is This a Great Subject or What?" You may choose to assign topics to your students.
- Once students select a subject, have them generate their own questions about it. Encourage them to ask for help if they need it.
- Read pages 120-121 as an overview of the information-gathering process. Discuss looking for information at home, at school, and in the community. Talk about the note card/gathering grid options. You may want to do a large gathering grid or model the use of note cards with the whole class.
- Direct children back and forth between the grid (page 121) and the model report (page 123). You might say, "Let's look at this fact on the grid—75-80 feet long and 40 feet high. Where do you find it in the report?" This will help students understand how to use the grid (or note cards). Students can record their questions on either of the blackline masters "Gathering Grid" or "Note Cards."

Writing a Classroom Report (pages 122-125)
- Have the children reread the model report, noticing the beginning, middle, and ending. The activity "Hook Your Reader" will help students write a good opening paragraph. Remind them that facts about one idea—size, for example—should all be in the same paragraph. Ask what makes John's ending good.
- Student models illustrate the "list poem" and "story" options. For published examples of these forms, see the "Reading/Writing Connection" at the end of this unit. For a discussion of oral reports, see "Giving Oral Reports" (pages 228-229) in the handbook.

A Closer Look at
Unit Masters

The type and number of masters vary from unit to unit. For example, the masters for the "The Forms of Writing" extended units address different stages in the development of the students' writing.

Planning Master ....➤

Checking Master ......

Writing Master ......➤

Name _____

Gathering Grid

DIRECTIONS: Write your subject and your questions in the boxes. Label your sources at the top. Write the answer to each question. (See page 121 in *Write Away* for an example.)

	SUBJECT	SOURCE	SOURCE
QUESTIONS			

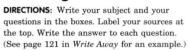

Name _____

Hook Your Reader

You need to write a good opening sentence to hook your readers. Two examples are given.

DIRECTIONS: Write two different opening sentences for your report. (1) Use a question. (2) Use an important fact.

Use a Question

What's the longest, tallest, and heaviest dinosaur that ever lived?

Your Turn: _____

_____

_____

Use an Important Fact

Brachiosaurus was taller than a four-story building.

Your Turn: _____

_____

_____

 Read both of your sentences to a friend. Ask which one works best.

62 *Writing Reports*   © Great Source. All rights reserved.

Name _____

Make Your Mystery Shine

DIRECTIONS: Follow these four steps to revise and proofread your mystery. After you finish each step, color in the triangle.

△ **Step One:** Read your story to yourself. Ask these questions:
  ✔ Did I put in some clues?
  ✔ Did I solve the problem?

△ **Step Two:** Read your story to a friend. Ask these questions:
  ✔ What is your favorite part?
  ✔ What ideas do you have for pictures?

△ **Step Three:** Polish your mystery.
  ✔ Check for capital letters and end punctuation.
  ✔ Check to see that you indented each time someone new speaks. (Did you use quotation marks?)
  ✔ Check your spelling.

△ **Step Four:** Make a neat copy of your story, including pictures.

© Great Source. All rights reserved.   *Writing Mysteries* **87**

---

182   *Program Overview*

A Closer Look at
Practice Workshops

The *SourceBook* workshop activities are designed to provide instruction and practice in basic proofreading and language skills. These activity sheets can be assigned individually, when students need information about a specific skill. A series of related activity sheets can also be implemented to explore a major topic like punctuation or parts of speech.

Opening copy leads students into the activity.

Instructions are clearly identified.

Name _____

Using Nouns

A **noun** names a person, a place, or a thing.

Person	Place	Thing
student	house	cake
friend	mall	fishing pole

A   Write what each word is: "person," "place," or "thing." Add two nouns of your own.

1. policeman   _____person_____
2. library   _____place_____
3. hammer   _____thing_____
4. teacher   _____person_____
5. pencil   _____thing_____
6. store   _____place_____
7. _____   _____
8. _____   _____

Understanding Our Language **79**

B   Write N if the word is a noun. Write X if the word is not a noun. Add two words of your own.

_N_ 1. paper	_X_ 4. bring	_X_ 7. and
_X_ 2. go	_N_ 5. girl	___ 8. _____
_N_ 3. bee	_N_ 6. store	___ 9. _____

C   Underline the noun in each sentence.

1. The <u>bus</u> is yellow.
2. The <u>spider</u> jumped.
3. This <u>game</u> is hard.
4. Look at the <u>duck</u>!
5. The <u>sky</u> looks pretty.
6. A <u>friend</u> called.

KEEP GOING   Write a sentence about your favorite place. Then underline the nouns in your sentence.

_____

_____

_____

80   *Understanding Our Language*

Many workshops include a follow-up activity.

A Closer Look at
Minilessons

Most of the minilessons address usage, mechanics, and grammar skills covered in the "Proofreader's Guide," and others focus on information found in the "Student Almanac." The minilessons can be used to introduce or review a basic skill when the need arises. Most minilessons can be completed in 10-15 minutes. They work especially well in writing-workshop classrooms.

Directions are clearly stated. ············▶

Some minilessons include examples to help students.

Checking Mechanics Minilessons

Dear Uncle Mike ················ **Capital Letters**

OPEN your handbook to page 70. **READ** the note from Sarah to Uncle Mike. Now **PRETEND** Sarah is talking instead of writing. **FILL IN** the blanks below with Sarah's words. Use a capital letter for Sarah's first word in each sentence. **SEE** page 255 in your handbook for help.

1. Sarah said, " Thank you for the calculator ."

2. Sarah said, " You always know what I need
_____ !"

3. " Now I can check my math homework
_____ ," said Sarah.

I like holidays. ················ **Capital Letters**

WRITE sentences about two or three of your favorite holidays. **TELL** what you like best about each holiday. Be sure to **USE** capitals letters correctly. **SEE** page 256 in your handbook.

Example: I love the heart cookies Grandma bakes for Valentine's Day.

Checking Mechanics Minilessons **111**

A Closer Look at
MUG Shot Sentences

MUG Shot Sentences come in two varieties. In the focused sentences, students concentrate on one proofreading skill at a time. In the proofreading sentences, students address two different types of errors. All sentences are designed for daily proofreading practice.

Focused Sentences ·······▸

Focused SENTENCES

* **Commas – Between a City and a State**

  Katie lives in Milford‸Michigan.

* **Commas – Between a City and a State**

  Disney World is in Orlando‸Florida.

* **Commas – Between a City and a State**

  Annie can't wait to go to San Antonio‸Texas.

* **Commas – Between a City and a State**

  Would you like to visit Friendly‸West Virginia?

* **Commas – Between a City and a State**

  Do many writers live in Pencil Bluff‸Arkansas?

136 *MUG Shot Sentences*

Proofreading SENTENCES

Zebras

* **Capitalization, End Punctuation**

  Z   A

  ✗ebras live in large herds in ✗frica‸

* **Commas, Quotation Marks**

  Grandpa said‸ “Baby zebras weigh about 70 pounds. ”

* **Quotation Marks, Capitalization**

  “ T   ”

  ✗hey are called foals, the zookeeper added.

* **Apostrophes, End Punctuation**

  Each zebra’s stripes form a different pattern‸

* **Using the Right Word, End Punctuation**

               hair

  Do zebras have brown ✗a̶r̶e̶ on their backs‸?

160 *MUG Shot Sentences*

◂······· **Proofreading Sentences**